SO, A CELIAC IS COMING FOR DINNER!

RECIPES AND TIPS
FOR EVERYDAY PEOPLE TO PROVIDE SAFE
FOODS FOR THOSE AVOIDING GLUTEN

Photography by Kendal Vanden Berg and Linda Vanden Berg
Graphic Design by Linda Vanden Berg

For additional books by CreativeFish,
please visit www.creativefish.ca

This book is
dedicated to all
the celiacs who
continually hear
these words.

"You're so lucky to get a whole bowl of ice cream to yourself?" as they eat their same sized cone. - "What do you mean you can't eat these cookies I made just for you? Is your diet more important?"

- "Are you still doing your wheat diet?" - "I made you Rice Krispies squares, Rice is gluten-free right?" - "All gluten-free food is terrible." - "I know exactly what that's like, because I'm a vegetarian."

"At least you don't have to be tempted by all this food!" - "The stuffing was inside the turkey, so the outside should be fine!"

"It's not like it can kill you!" - "Don't bring anything!! It'll all be safe!" - "Are you just doing it cause it's trendy?" - "I paid $9 for your gluten-free bread, despite you being sick at least you could appreciate that!"

"Suck it up, you're overly dramatic. A crumb isn't going to kill you. You'll just throw up and move on". - "You can just pick the croutons off". - "I think it's just in your head"

"It only has a tbsp of mushroom soup .. it'll be fine". - "Can't you just cheat?" - "I would kill myself if I couldn't eat bread". - "A little bit won't hurt you"

TABLE OF
CONTENTS

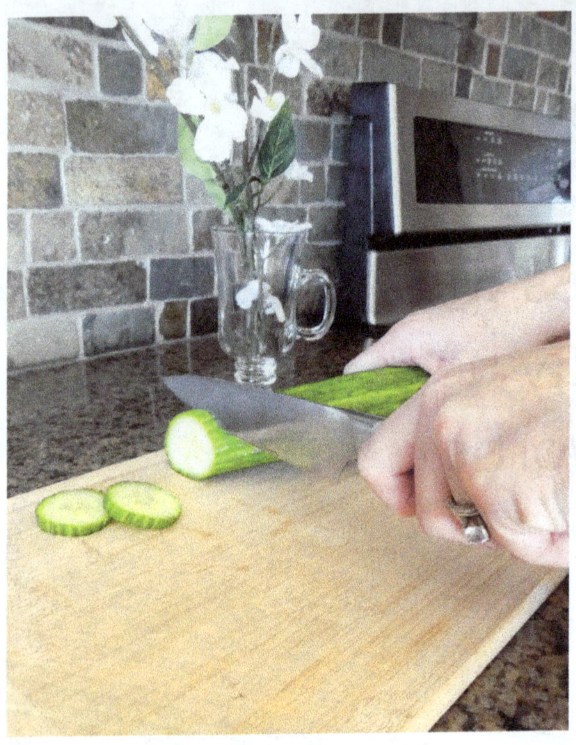

I am not a professional chef, but I have been baking and cooking for decades. After being diagnosed as a teen with type 1 diabetes and then 10 years ago dealing with celiac disease, I have learned very quickly how to cook and handle gluten-free food safely for myself, my family, and many others.

I love to experiment with new ideas and discover new foods.

This isn't a typical cookbook. Although it does have recipes and tips for making food, the focus of this book is to provide help and ideas for people that need to make food "gluten-free"' safely for an occasional reason, but they don't need to do it regularly.

INTRODUCTION

Creating this book has been a long-term project. I stopped working on it numerous times because I was concerned that many people may state it was inappropriate for non gluten-free people to make gluten-free food as it may be done in an unsafe environment. I was also concerned about scaring someone from even attempting to prepare food for a gluten-intolerant person, especially after reading the first part of this book, as it may seem daunting and the repercussions of a mistake could be severe.

However, I continually encountered situations where we were at a friend's house, an event, or offered something **'Gluten Free' (GF)** only to learn it wasn't. Often the host/baker wasn't even aware what they were offering contained gluten or that it was cooked around contaminants. There are lots of books and online recipes on how to cook gluten-free, but I often wished there was something for non gluten-free people explaining how to make something safe for those gluten-intolerant but more on an occasional basis rather than all the time.

I am also a member of many celiac-related, online groups where many people mention dreading the holidays or family get-togethers. There are many reasons to dread family get-togethers, so I don't think eating food should be one of those reasons. 

Therefore, I decided it was worth finishing this cookbook as I was sure I could create something beneficial for anyone cooking for gluten-avoiding people. I'll admit I still have unpleasant visions about someone being glutened by a recipe. I'm worried that someone would not follow the precautions, but say they did. I realize though that I need to look beyond this concern and focus on the benefits. I believe I am successful by combining simple information about how and why there is a need to avoid gluten. Then I add to this with recipes that anyone can make, including specific instructions on how to make it safe for gluten avoiders.

For those intimidated by this information, please remember preparing food for someone is more than just a meal. It can create a meaningful and nurturing experience that goes beyond satisfying hunger. It can foster relationships, show care and love, be a cultural experience, provide comfort, and create memories that last a lifetime. Use any anxiety you may have to focus on the steps and follow precautions and you can be successful. Just be open with your gluten-free guest.

 Although there are always risks for gluten avoiders when eating out, I WOULD NOT BE WRITING THIS COOKBOOK IF MAKING FOOD SAFE WAS NOT POSSIBLE. Just be cautious and follow my instructions and you can make a safe, enjoyable dish.

MEET THE AUTHOR

Without devaluing real chefs, I'm what you would call a self-proclaimed amateur chef. I have been baking and cooking for decades, but without any formal cooking education. So, what can I offer? After being diagnosed with type 1 diabetes as a teenager (many, many years ago), I learned quickly how to cook and handle food and rapidly fell in love with cooking.

Then my life changed about 10 years ago when celiac disease joined our family. We were shattered by the news initially and the belief that good eating was in the past. However, it was agreed it was safer as a family for everyone to go gluten-free. Therefore, I did A LOT of research, had discussions with dieticians and nutritionists, read many books, did heaps of online research, and did lots of hands-on experimentation.

I quickly acquired a renewed passion for providing my family with appetizing gluten-free food and showing others avoiding gluten doesn't mean denying oneself amazing food.

Presently, I devote a great deal of time to exploration in the kitchen, the discovery of new foods and distinctive methods of preparation and LOTS of trial and error.

Recently we started food processing as we now make most of our own sausages and lunch meat AND it's all GLUTEN-FREE. I'd like to say I'm successful. My husband and kids aren't complaining and family and friends are continually asking for recipes. I have learned a lot and hope to share this with others.

IS THIS A COOKBOOK?

Yes and No! This isn't a typical cookbook. Yes, it has recipes and tips for making food, but the focus of this book is to provide help and ideas for people that need to make food 'gluten-free' for an occasional reason, but they don't need to do it on a regular basis.

- Maybe your child comes home from school asking you to make a treat for the class, but one of the kids cannot have gluten.

- A friend you haven't seen in years is coming for a visit, but you heard she's avoiding gluten now.

- Maybe you need to bring a dish to a work event and someone has told you a co-worker can't have gluten.

- It's holiday time!! But your daughter is bringing her new boyfriend for dinner and he has celiac disease.

AAUUUGGHHHH!!!   What do you do?

Whether it's a long-time friend, someone you just met, a co-worker, a passing acquaintance or maybe it's even a family member, eventually it's bound to happen. You need to make a snack or dish for someone that can't have gluten.

So now what?? Do you even know what gluten is? Maybe you know nothing. Maybe you know exactly what gluten is, but you don't know how many areas of your kitchen could hide gluten. Maybe you know some things about gluten but still need just a little help. Regardless of your knowledge base, this book is ideal for you.

Whatever the situation, it seems there are many people avoiding gluten these days and regardless of whether they choose to eat gluten-free or are required to eat gluten-free, there is likely to come a time when you need to make a snack or a safe meal. Where do you start?

WHO AVOIDS GLUTEN?

In simple terms, **gluten is a protein found in wheat, rye and barley that acts as a binder, or 'glue' that holds products together.**

Let's start by thinking about the people that avoid gluten. I have separated the main groups of people that avoid gluten into 4 simple groups. For more detail about a particular group, please feel free to research more yourself.

It is important to know that regardless of why the person is avoiding gluten, making them a safe, delicious meal or snack is equally important. The main differences between each group are the severity of reactions and the precautions that are needed. Much more care is needed for celiac disease than may be needed for a choice avoidance of gluten.

Sometimes you can ask your gluten-avoiding guest how severe their reaction is or how cautious they are about eating out and take whatever steps are necessary. I will try to highlight some of the different methods you may be able to use whether avoiding gluten is a necessity or a choice.

1)   Those with Celiac Disease

For the first group of gluten avoiders, you have people with **celiac disease (or coeliac disease** as it is known in some countries). What exactly is celiac disease?

There are many good books and articles on the internet that can provide you with a lot of detail about celiac disease therefore, I'll stay brief.

Simply put, celiac disease is a condition where the small intestine is damaged by ingesting gluten. The immediate damage to the intestine is symptoms such as diarrhea, headaches, abdominal pain, nausea, vomiting, gas, etc. However, continual exposure can permanently damage the intestines and result in the body being unable to absorb nutrients which can lead to longer-term complications like malnutrition and cancer.

This is not a fad diet or a personal choice! Someone with celiac disease must avoid gluten for their lifetime. Even if the celiac person has no visible symptoms there is always the potential for long-term harm to the intestines.

2) People who are Gluten Intolerant

People who are gluten intolerant will likely have all the same reactions to consuming gluten as a celiac, but there is normally no long-term damage to the small intestines. Sometimes you hear people say they have a gluten sensitivity. This is the group they would fit in.

People in both groups 1 and 2, can sometimes have no visible reactions, but more commonly they have somewhere between an immediate, short-term, but high-intensity reaction OR a slow onset, less intense but long-lasting attack. Always remember that for some, just because you may not see any visual signs of a reaction, there can still be damage on the inside. Therefore it is vital to be careful no matter where the person fits on the spectrum.

3) Choice Avoidance

There are many people who choose to not eat gluten as a lifestyle choice. Although it is still important to respect the choice this guest has made with their eating habits, the concern for cross-contact from an outside source of gluten is less important.

4) Allergy

Although many people with celiac disease will say they have a gluten allergy, celiac disease is NOT an allergy. In today's world, people pay more attention and take greater precautions for an allergy, therefore the word is used for this reason. However, some people must avoid wheat as an allergy. They normally eat gluten-free, but in addition must be careful as some products, although safe for a celiac, may still contain a trace amount of wheat and cause reactions and anaphylaxis.

PLEASE don't think it is not dangerous because you can't die from eating something with gluten. Many people do end up in the hospital due to the severity of their reactions. Despite the fact the reaction may not be as immediately life-threatening as an allergy, repeated exposure can lead to malnutrition, stomach cancer, and death.

WHAT PRODUCTS HAVE GLUTEN?

The easiest way to think about what has gluten is to say anything made from flour such as Breads, Pasta, Crackers, Muffins, Buns, etc. However, there is much more.

Barley, rye, triticale, farro, farina, graham flour, semolina, durum, einkorn, emmer, spelt, kamut, wheat, wheat starch, wheat bran, wheat germ, and cracked wheat ALL CONTAIN GLUTEN in their natural state.

To identify what has gluten, an easy starting point is to check the label for BROW ingredients. BROW being an acronym for **B**arley, **R**ye, regular **O**ats, and **W**heat.

In the USA, if wheat or any wheat-related ingredients are included in the food product the ingredient label should clearly show it contains wheat. However, barley and rye are not identified as major allergens and therefore, do not have to be identified on the label. For example, malt is normally derived from barley, but as it is not an allergen, it doesn't have to state anything more than malt.

In Canada, Australia, and the UK, gluten of any kind must be stated in plain language on the label and cannot be 'hidden' behind a name like malt. For example, if malt is made from barley, it must clearly state it in brackets after malt or in the 'contains' area of the label.

Therefore, some extra ingredients need to be avoided in the USA. These will be addressed in future pages.

Luckily in today's world, any food packaged for sale must include an ingredient label. This allows us to check to see if there is anything we don't want to consume in the food item.

Since this book is focused more on people that don't know the ins and outs of avoiding gluten, I am going to err on the side of safety when selecting safe gluten-free food.

Cross-contamination (or the more correct term of cross-contact), will be covered in another chapter, but you have to be careful with products like oats and corn. These don't contain gluten themselves, but they can sometimes be dangerous.

READING LABELS

How to safely read a food label for gluten!

Labels and ingredient lists are much clearer than they used to be. As already discussed in the previous chapter, in Canada, Australia, and the UK, it is a law to use simple language regarding allergens on the label. They cannot be hidden behind other names or undisclosed sources.

These countries also take steps cautioning against oats, which are a high risk for cross-contact due to exposure to gluten during harvest, transport, or while being processed in factories. As well, some caution against cornmeal or corn flour. If they are listed in the first 2 ingredients and it doesn't state gluten-free, then the recommendation is to avoid them. Just to note that cornstarch is deemed safe as it is highly processed.

PLEASE NOTE: In the USA/Canada, cornmeal is a coarse flour ground from dried corn. It is gritty. Corn flour is finely ground corn and then cornstarch is the end result of processing corn flour to extract only the starch. However, in many other countries, cornstarch is known as cornflour and corn flour is known as cornmeal. Simply put, in the UK/Australia cornflour = US/Canada corn starch (which is safe) and UK/Australia cornmeal = US/Canada corn flour (which has warnings). In my diagrams, please understand that the terms used are North American terms so adjust accordingly to the product in your country.

Labeling laws in the USA are different. Wheat cannot be hidden but other allergens can be hidden. As well, the FDA doesn't allow descriptions in the ingredient list like "gluten-free oats". Sometimes, it is up to the shopper to interpret the labels. **Understand that a lack of allergens on a USA label does NOT mean that the product is gluten-free.**

Therefore, the following pages outline a simplified diagram for someone who is not as familiar with looking for gluten. The first diagram is targeted at shoppers in countries like Canada, the United Kingdom, and Australia. The second diagram is focused more on shoppers in the United States. Both diagrams are designed to err on the side of safety when dealing with a more controversial item. If you are not sure which diagram to use, go with the USA version as it is better to be overly cautious, than under cautious.

As mentioned before, since some gluten sources can be hidden in the USA, you do need to avoid some products that may actually be safe due to the fact you simply don't know. A regular gluten avoider will learn much more about reading labels, but I am leaning towards safety for this Cookbook. Better to be safe than sorry.

One last thing to remember is **labels can change**. Just because something was 'gluten-free' once, doesn't mean you don't have to always check. Ingredients can change, manufacturers can decide to change their production process or maybe source ingredients from new distributors. Therefore, it is important you **check the label every time you buy a product**. The label always overrides the information online.

The difference between **gluten-free** and **certified gluten-free**:

"**Gluten-free**" means the item can't contain more than the government-allowed amount of gluten AND the manufacturer has followed steps to prevent gluten cross-contact. In the USA however, gluten testing occurs on the ingredients used before processing, not on the final item produced. The USA regulation states that the manufacturer is responsible for continued follow-up testing and the FDA only does spot checks and as a result, many manufacturers don't continue testing for gluten. Therefore, despite the fact no gluten ingredients are included, the final product may have gluten above acceptable levels and may not be safe for those gluten intolerant.

"**Certified gluten-free**" means the finished item has also been independently tested by a 3rd party for the presence of gluten. This process is usually audited and retested at specified intervals. Gluten-free certification can provide a significant sense of relief for individuals following a gluten-free diet. Most gluten avoiders are much more confident in certified gluten-free labeling than just a gluten-free statement.

Reading cereal labels - Many cereals don't contain any gluten ingredients. Lucky Charms, Crispix, and Cheerios are a few examples with NO gluten-containing ingredients. However, they all contain high-risk ingredients like oats or corn that may have had cross-contact with gluten.   As the words gluten-free do not appear on these cereals, they should be avoided due to this risk.

To be safe for your guests - **only cereals that state gluten-free** should be used. If you are in the USA, you should also ensure that either the box is certified gluten-free or somewhere on the box it states specifically that gluten-free oats/corn were used.
Cheerios do state gluten-free on the box in the USA only. In Canada, they are not considered gluten-free as the oats are not certified gluten-free and some boxes test above the acceptable level of gluten. Some people may take the chance, but since you are buying for someone else, I suggest you buy only certified gluten-free cereals.

Note that some products can be certified gluten-free, but there could still be a 'may contain' wheat warning. This warning is for allergies to wheat. A product can be certified gluten-free and safe for those that avoid gluten as it is within the acceptable level, but it still contains enough wheat to potentially cause an issue for someone with an allergy.

How to Read a Label for Gluten (Non USA)

I suggest you take a photo on your phone or make a copy of this diagram before going shopping.

① Is there a **"Gluten-Free"** claim ? — YES →

↓ NO

② **Read the ingredients** on label. Does this item have any BROW [Barley, Rye, Oats (that are Non-certified GF) or Wheat] OR does it have cornmeal or corn flour * in first 2 ingredients?

* Please see note on page 16, regarding cornflours.

YES →

↓ NO

③ Is there a **"Contains" statement?** As above, you are looking for any reference to any BROW ingredients.

YES →

↓ NO

④ Does this product have a **"May contain"** wheat or a **made in a facility** that also processes wheat statement? -> these statements are optional, but if they exist, then this item is NOT safe.

YES →

↓ NO

If the product has no gluten-free claim, but there are also no BROW (Barley, Rye, Oats (regular) or Wheat) ingredients in either ingredients list OR 'contains' OR 'may contain' AND corn flour and cornmeal are not listed in the first 2 ingredients, then this product is

SAFE TO USE

How to Read a Label for Gluten (USA)

I suggest you take a photo on your phone or make a copy of this diagram prior to going shopping.

① Is there a **"Gluten Free"** claim ?

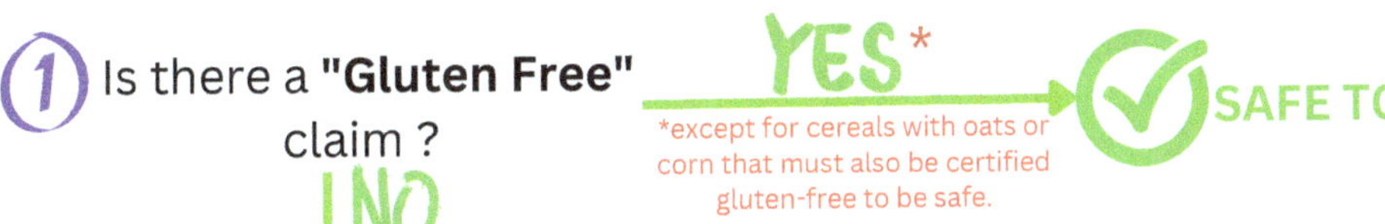

↓ NO

② **Read the ingredients** on label. Does this item have any BROW [Barley, Rye, Oats (that are Non-certified GF) or Wheat] or does it have cornmeal or corn flour in first 2 ingredients? ✱ **Please see below for extra ingredients!**

↓ NO

③ Is there a **"Contains" statement?** As above, you are looking for any reference to any BROW ingredients

↓ NO

④ Does this product have a **"May contain"** wheat or a **made in a facility** that also processes wheat statement?   -> these statements are optional, but if they exist, then this item is NOT safe.

↓ NO

If the product has no gluten-free claim, but there are also no BROW (Barley, Rye, Oats (regular) or Wheat) ingredients in the ingredients list OR 'contains' OR 'may contain' AND corn flour and cornmeal are not listed in the first 2 ingredients, then this product is

SAFE TO USE

✱ **EXTRA UNSAFE INGREDIENTS:** Bulgur, Couscous, Triticale, Farro, Farina, Graham flour, Semolina, Durum, Einkorn, Emmer, Malt, Seitan, Spelt, Kamut, Wheat starch, Wheat bran, Wheat germ and Cracked wheat, if they are not specified as being gluten-free.   As well, you need to avoid vague terms like Smoke Flavoring ; Brewer's Yeast ; Yeast Extract ; Rice Syrup and Seasonings (without a sub ingredient list) as all of these MAY be derived from wheat or barley and if the package doesn't state they are gluten-free, they need to be avoided.

Food Label Examples

For this example, I have 2 ingredient labels for a Macaron. One is the authentic, traditional cookie/biscuit and the other is a cheaper, generic one. I will specify that both packages did NOT include any reference to the product being gluten-free.

REMEMBER TO READ THE LABEL EVERY TIME

Example #1

INGREDIENTS:
Powdered Sugar, Organic Almond Meal (Gluten-free), Sugar, Butter, Pasteurized Egg White.

Is this cookie/biscuit safe? Following the appropriate 'How to Read a Label' diagram on the previous pages

① **Is there a gluten-free claim?** - there was NO gluten-free claim on the packaging so continuing to go through the diagram let's move on to

② **Reading the ingredients**. It does clearly state almond meal is gluten-free so we know it's likely all gluten-free but don't assume. Let's continue looking for any other BROW (Barley, Rye, Oats, or Wheat) ingredients or corn flour or cornmeal. Moving on you can see there are NO other concerning Ingredients from either diagram. Moving along

③ **Any Contains statement?** - NONE found. Moving on to

④ **Any 'May contain' statement?** - NONE found. Therefore this product is SAFE TO EAT for those Gluten Intolerant.

Example #2

This is a label from another package of cookie or biscuits (Macarons) so again we are going to follow the diagram on the previous page.

Is this cookie/biscuit safe?

① As stated, there was **NO gluten-free claim** on the packaging. Continuing down through the diagrams from the previous page, let's move on to

② **Reading the ingredients**. Looking through through the list of ingredients you will see Glucose Syrup (Wheat) and Malted Barley Extract. These <u>are</u> BROW Ingredients - Barley, Rye, Oats or Wheat. .

There is no further reason to continue as the answer is YES, therefore moving right with the arrow, this automatically means this cookie/biscuit is **NOT SAFE TO EAT.**

You can see it also has a 'Contains' showing Wheat

INGREDIENTS: SUGAR, ALMOND POWDER, EGG WHITES, CREAM, CORN STARCH, BUTTER (CULTURED CREAM), RASPBERRIES, WHITE CHOCOLATE (SUGAR, COCOA BUTTER, DRY WHOLE MILK, SOY LECITHIN, NATURAL FLAVOR), GLUCOSE SYRUP (WHEAT), CHOCOLATE (COCOA MASS, SUGAR, COCOA BUTTER, SOY LECITHIN), CHOCOLATE (COCOA MASS, SUGAR, SOY LECITHIN), ALMOND PUREE, EGGS, LEMON, RAPESEED OIL, LEMON JUICE, NONFAT DRY MILK, PISTACHIOS, NATURAL FLAVORS, WATER, DEHYDRATED BEET (COLOR), MALTED BARLEY EXTRACT, PECTIN, COCOA BUTTER, CARAMELIZED SUGAR, SPIRULINA EXTRACT (COLOR), COFFEE, XANTHAN GUM, AGAR-AGAR, TURMERIC OLEORESIN (COLOR), INVERT SUGAR, EXHAUSTED VANILLA SEEDS, CITRIC ACID, CARRAGEENAN, ASCORBIC ACID.

CONTAINS MILK, EGGS, ALMONDS, PISTACHIOS, WHEAT AND SOY. MAY CONTAIN TRACES OF HAZELNUT AND COCONUT.

20

Example #3 - Hot Dogs #1

"Hot dogs are just meat, how can they contain gluten?"

Is this Hot Dog safe to eat? In this case, there is ① **NO** gluten-free claim. Next step ② Read the Ingredients. Since there are **NO** BROW (Barley, Rye, Oats, or Wheat) ingredients found, there is no cornmeal or corn flour or any additional concerning ingredients for USA labels, we can continue following the diagram. ③ There is **NO** 'Contains' and ④ **NO** 'May Contain' statement, therefore this product is SAFE TO EAT.

Example #4 - Hot Dogs #2

Ingredients: Pork • Mechanically separated chicken • Water • Enriched wheat flour • Salt • Potassium lactate • Corn starch • Sodium phosphate • Sugars (dextrose) • Natural smoke flavour • Onion powder • Sodium erythorbate • Sodium diacetate • Garlic powder • Spices • Sodium nitrite • Polysorbate 80
Contains: Wheat
May Contain: Milk • Eggs

Is this Hot Dog Safe to eat? In this case, ① the packaging did not state anything about it being gluten-free. So the next step is to ② Read the Ingredients. Since there <u>are</u> BROW (Barley, Rye, Oats, or Wheat) ingredients i.e. wheat flour, this product is **NOT SAFE TO EAT**. **Please note** for those in the USA, this product is also unsafe as it also contains Smoke Flavor which may contain gluten and should also be avoided.

You can also see it is clearly stated in the Contains section that it contains Wheat.

Example #5 - Licorice

Is this Licorice Safe to eat? It's candy, it should be gluten-free right? Wrong! In this case ① the packaging did not state anything about it being gluten-free. So the next step is ② Read the ingredients. Since <u>YES</u> there are BROW (Barley, Rye, Oats or Wheat) ingredients i.e. wheat flour, this product is **NOT SAFE TO EAT**.

This is a tougher example as there are no bold ingredients or any Contains or May contain statement. However, wheat flour is legible.   DO NOT USE!

Let's see if you can figure out which of these products are safe.
Look on the following page for the answers.
No peeking!

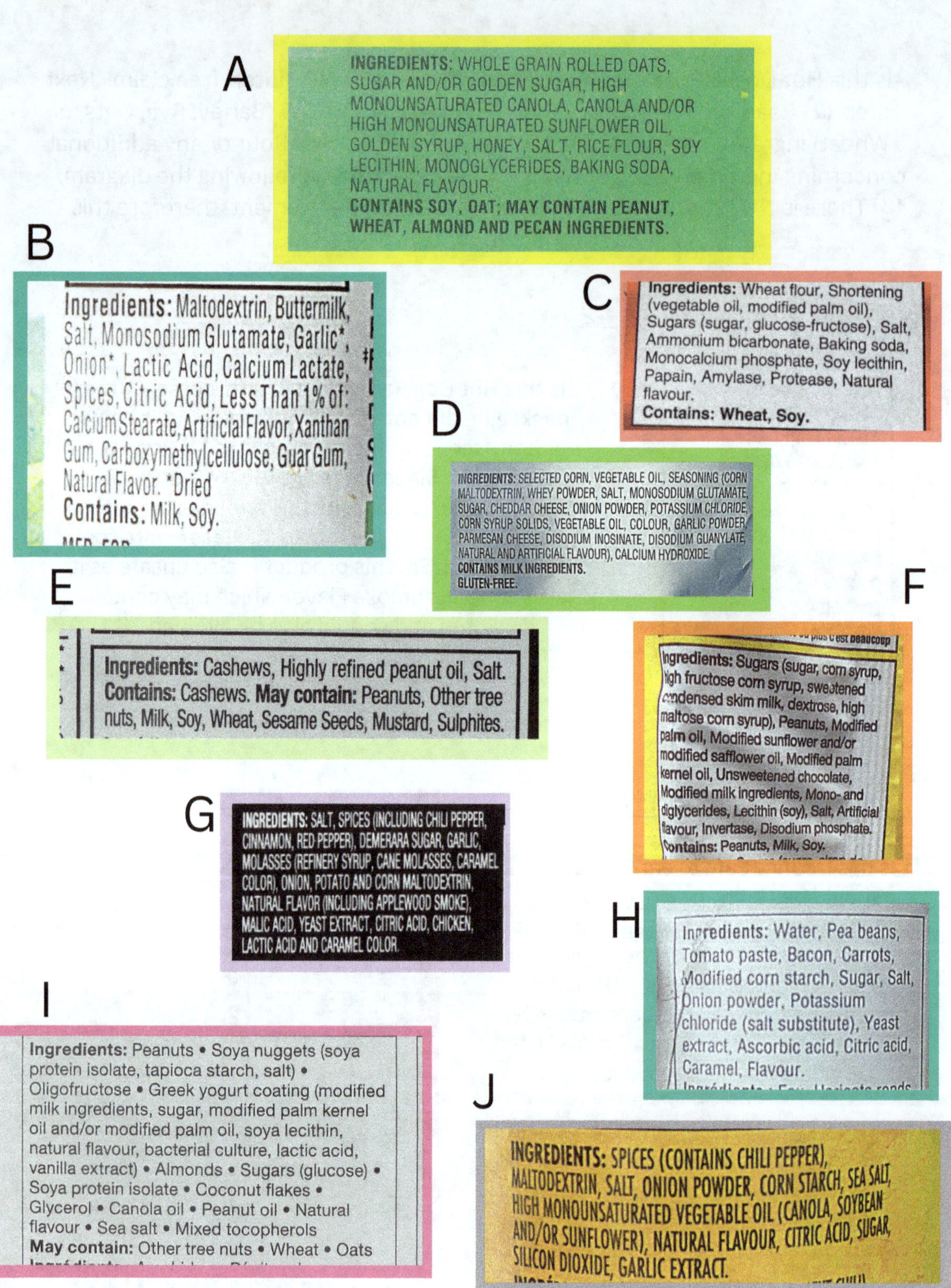

Here are the answers to previous page!

SAFE - B,D,F,**G,H**,J   ## NOT SAFE - A,C,E,**G,H**,I

Please note that 'G' and 'H' are under both Safe and Unsafe. See the explanation within the boxes below.

A

INGREDIENTS: WHOLE GRAIN ROLLED OATS, SUGAR AND/OR GOLDEN SUGAR, HIGH MONOUNSATURATED CANOLA, CANOLA AND/OR HIGH MONOUNSATURATED SUNFLOWER OIL, GOLDEN SYRUP, HONEY, SALT, RICE FLOUR, SOY LECITHIN, MONOGLYCERIDES, BAKING SODA, NATURAL FLAVOUR.
CONTAINS SOY, OAT; MAY CONTAIN PEANUT, WHEAT, ALMOND AND PECAN INGREDIENTS.

A) Step 1 - No gluten-free statement, Step 2 - it does NOT have certified gluten-free oats so this is **NOT SAFE**. It also has a 'May Contain' statement but has already been determined to be unsafe.

B

Ingredients: Maltodextrin, Buttermilk, Salt, Monosodium Glutamate, Garlic*, Onion*, Lactic Acid, Calcium Lactate, Spices, Citric Acid, Less Than 1% of: Calcium Stearate, Artificial Flavor, Xanthan Gum, Carboxymethylcellulose, Guar Gum, Natural Flavor. *Dried
Contains: Milk, Soy.

B) Step 1 - No gluten-free statement, Step 2 - No BROW ingredients or corn, Step 3 - No 'Contains' BROW, Step 4 - No 'May contain' statement - This item is **SAFE**

C

Ingredients: Wheat flour, Shortening (vegetable oil, modified palm oil), Sugars (sugar, glucose-fructose), Salt, Ammonium bicarbonate, Baking soda, Monocalcium phosphate, Soy lecithin, Papain, Amylase, Protease, Natural flavour.
Contains: Wheat, Soy.

C) Step 1 - No gluten-free statement, Step 2 - it does have Wheat so this is **NOT SAFE**

D

INGREDIENTS: SELECTED CORN, VEGETABLE OIL, SEASONING (CORN MALTODEXTRIN, WHEY POWDER, SALT, MONOSODIUM GLUTAMATE, SUGAR, CHEDDAR CHEESE, ONION POWDER, POTASSIUM CHLORIDE, CORN SYRUP SOLIDS, VEGETABLE OIL, COLOUR, GARLIC POWDER, PARMESAN CHEESE, DISODIUM INOSINATE, DISODIUM GUANYLATE, NATURAL AND ARTIFICIAL FLAVOUR), CALCIUM HYDROXIDE.
CONTAINS MILK INGREDIENTS.
GLUTEN-FREE.

D) Step 1 - It has a gluten-free statement. This product is **SAFE**

E

Ingredients: Cashews, Highly refined peanut oil, Salt.
Contains: Cashews. **May contain:** Peanuts, Other tree nuts, Milk, Soy, Wheat, Sesame Seeds, Mustard, Sulphites.

E) Step 1 - No gluten-free statement, Step 2 - it has No concerning BROW, Step 3 - It does not have a concerning :'Contains" statement. Step 4 - It **does** have a 'May contain' Wheat. This item is **NOT SAFE**.

F

Ingredients: Sugars (sugar, corn syrup, high fructose corn syrup, sweetened condensed skim milk, dextrose, high maltose corn syrup), Peanuts, Modified palm oil, Modified sunflower and/or modified safflower oil, Modified palm kernel oil, Unsweetened chocolate, Modified milk ingredients, Mono- and diglycerides, Lecithin (soy), Salt, Artificial flavour, Invertase, Disodium phosphate.
Contains: Peanuts, Milk, Soy.

F) Step 1 - No gluten-free statement, Step 2 - No BROW ingredients Step 3 - No Contains BROW, Step 4 - No May contain statement - This item is **SAFE**

G

INGREDIENTS: SALT, SPICES (INCLUDING CHILI PEPPER, CINNAMON, RED PEPPER), DEMERARA SUGAR, GARLIC, MOLASSES (REFINERY SYRUP, CANE MOLASSES, CARAMEL COLOR), ONION, POTATO AND CORN MALTODEXTRIN, NATURAL FLAVOUR (INCLUDING APPLEWOOD SMOKE), MALIC ACID, YEAST EXTRACT, CITRIC ACID, CHICKEN, LACTIC ACID AND CARAMEL COLOR.

G) Step 1 - No gluten-free statement, Step 2 - No BROW ingredients or corn* Step 3 - No 'contains' statement, Step 4 - No 'May contain' statement - This item is **SAFE** outside the USA.

*However, in the US, Yeast Extract is one of the concerning ingredients that may include gluten, therefore it is safer to **AVOID THIS PRODUCT.**

H

Ingredients: Water, Pea beans, Tomato paste, Bacon, Carrots, Modified corn starch, Sugar, Salt, Onion powder, Potassium chloride (salt substitute), Yeast extract, Ascorbic acid, Citric acid, Caramel Flavour.

H) Step 1 - No gluten-free statement. Step 2 - No BROW ingredients or corn flour or cornmeal* Step 3 - No 'Contains' statement, Step 4 - No 'May contain' statement - This item is **SAFE** outside the USA.

*However, in the US, Yeast Extract is one of the concerning ingredients that may include gluten, therefore it is safer to **AVOID THIS PRODUCT.**

I

I) Step 1 - no gluten-free statement, Step 2 - it has no concerning BROW ingredients or corn, Step 3 - It does not have a 'Contains' statement, Step 4 It **does** have a 'May contain' Wheat. This item is **NOT** safe.

Ingredients: Peanuts • Soya nuggets (soya protein isolate, tapioca starch, salt) • Oligofructose • Greek yogurt coating (modified milk ingredients, sugar, modified palm kernel oil and/or modified palm oil, soya lecithin, natural flavour, bacterial culture, lactic acid, vanilla extract) • Almonds • Sugars (glucose) • Soya protein isolate • Coconut flakes • Glycerol • Canola oil • Peanut oil • Natural flavour • Sea salt • Mixed tocopherols
May contain: Other tree nuts • Wheat • Oats

J

J) Step 1 - No gluten-free statement, Step 2 - No BROW ingredients and no concerning corn products, Step 3 - No 'Contains' statement, Step 4 - No 'May contain' statement - This item is **SAFE**

INGREDIENTS: SPICES (CONTAINS CHILI PEPPER), MALTODEXTRIN, SALT, ONION POWDER, CORN STARCH, SEA SALT, HIGH MONOUNSATURATED VEGETABLE OIL (CANOLA, SOYBEAN AND/OR SUNFLOWER), NATURAL FLAVOUR, CITRIC ACID, SUGAR, SILICON DIOXIDE, GARLIC EXTRACT.

More examples as Reading Labels is very important!

REMEMBER TO READ THE LABEL EVERY TIME

This label is easy to identify a gluten source. **NOT SAFE TO EAT**

INGREDIENTS: DRIED ONION, SPICES (BLACK PEPPER, CHILI PEPPER, PARSLEY, CELERY SEED, BASIL, BAY, MARJORAM, OREGANO, SAVORY, THYME, MUSTARD, CUMIN, ROSEMARY, CAYENNE PEPPER, CORIANDER), DRIED GARLIC, DRIED ORANGE PEEL, DRIED CARROT, DRIED TOMATO, DRIED RED BELL PEPPER, LEMON JUICE POWDER, CITRIC ACID, OIL OF LEMON.

This label is good and there are no concerning gluten sources. In the USA, the word Spices can be confusing as Seasonings is on the concerning list, but they are different. If there are any non-spice ingredients in Spices, such as starch, they must be included in the ingredients list by their common name. Whereas Seasonings are only a concern if they have no sub-ingredient list or if a gluten source is listed. Usually, just the word seasonings means it's mislabeled and should be avoided. This product however is **SAFE TO EAT**.

This label is easy to read as it only has a few ingredients. Although the ingredients are not a concern, it does state it is packaged in a facility that packages products containing Wheat so it has a 'May contain' statement. This product is **NOT SAFE**

INGREDIENTS: Salt, Maltodextrin, Dehydrated Garlic and Onion, Spice, Sunflower Oil, Disodium Inosinate and Disodium Guanylate, Natural Flavor.

Packaged in a facility that also packages products containing dairy, wheat, and soy.

Ingredients: Corn Maltodextrin, Salt, Buttermilk, Natural Flavors, Monosodium Glutamate, Garlic*, Spices, Less Than 2% of: Sodium Diacetate, Calcium Lactate, Onion*, Paprika, Xanthan Gum, Guar Gum, Paprika Extract, Soy Flour, Silicon Dioxide. *Dried
Contains: Milk, Soy.

There are no concerning gluten ingredients on this label. It also has a 'Contains' statement without WHEAT therefore, this product is **SAFE TO EAT**.

This label doesn't state gluten-free and although it doesn't show any gluten sources, corn meal is the first ingredient and as it may be unsafe due to cross-contact, it should be avoided. If it did state gluten-free somewhere on the bag it would be OK. Overall this product is **NOT SAFE TO EAT**

INGREDIENTS: CORN MEAL, HYDROGENATED VEGETABLE OIL, PROCESSED AGED CHEDDAR CHEESE SEASONING, LACTIC ACID, DISODIUM PHOSPHATE, SALT AND CERTIFIED COLOUR (CONTAINS TARTRAZINE).
CONTAINS: MILK.

INGREDIENTS: MALTODEXTRIN, SALT, GARLIC POWDER, POTATO STARCH, SUGAR, PARMESAN AND ROMANO CHEESES (PASTEURIZED MILK, CHEESE CULTURES, SALT, ENZYMES), SPINACH POWDER, PARSLEY, WHEY, BASIL, HYDROLYZED CORN PROTEIN, CORNSTARCH, HIGH OLEIC SUNFLOWER OIL, GARLIC, NATURAL FLAVORS, GUAR GUM, DISODIUM GUANYLATE, DISODIUM INOSINATE, SULFITES USED TO PROTECT QUALITY). MAY CONTAIN WHEAT AND SOY.

Although there are no concerning ingredients itself, this label clearly has a 'May contain' Wheat statement so this product is **NOT SAFE TO EAT**

HOW MUCH IS TOO MUCH?

So you just avoid anything with gluten right?
Unfortunately, it's not that easy.

Except for those avoiding gluten by choice, even the smallest amount of gluten can trigger a reaction. How small? This can be confusing to figure out and some people may be able to tolerate more than others. The official response is **- less than 10 mg of gluten per day. Therefore, if gluten was present in things you normally eat every day at levels less than 20 ppm (parts per million), exposure to gluten would remain below 10 mg per day.**

(Please note that Australia and NZ are even more restricted at < 3 ppm)

If you're like most people, that does NOT make it clear. Right?
SO.... let's put it in terms most people can visualize.

SKIP THIS PART if it hurts your brain AND JUMP to the **RESULTS** section below. Firstly, what is 20 PPM? - think of an extremely large bowl with a million pieces of rice and 20 are painted green, meaning the other 999,980 are white. Therefore, this bowl, has 20 ppm (parts per million) of green rice. That's an easy calculation, but it doesn't make it clear yet does it?

Using my advanced math skills 😉 to reduce this ratio even more, I get 1 green piece of rice in 50,000. The internet tells me there are many types of rice so 1 cup of rice can average between 5,000-10,000 pieces.

RESULTS

If gluten was green, 1 grain of green rice in 5-10 cups of white rice could cause issues for a gluten-intolerant person.

Another common way to think of it is a tiny crumb from a single piece of regular bread could cause issues for someone gluten intolerant.

Now picture how many tiny toast crumbs may already be sitting in your butter or margarine container at home!

And there are so many more places gluten can reside in your home.

Do you wipe your counters with a common dishcloth and/or towel? Particles and crumbs can stay in a dishcloth or towel and redistribute somewhere you don't want them.

When was the last time you cleaned out your cutlery drawer?. Take a look at how many crumbs are hiding along side your utensils used to serve and eat food?

What was the last thing you made in your Blender, Stand, or Hand mixer? Cookie/biscuits? Cake? Bread? Is there any flour or batter that may still be found on the underneath part of the machine? What about the parts that rotate, but can't be removed and cleaned like where the beaters attach to the machine?

Do you have a favorite cast iron fry pan? Do you know how many food particles can stay in the little indentations that make this such a wonderful pan to use?

Has your Teflon fry pan seen better days? Does it have a few wear marks or scratches? Gluten loves to hide in these little places and doesn't always wash out.

Do you have a wooden cutting board? Or a plastic type with deep grooves? Gluten particles can hide in the small scratches or grooves in many cutting boards.

Do you toast your bread? Or maybe throw a bun on the grill to warm and toast it before eating. How many tiny particles could be residing on the grill or in the toaster?

Have you baked lately with regular all-purpose wheat flour? Did you know flour particles can float in the air for 24-48 hours? That means that the cookie/biscuits you made yesterday might have caused flour to be floating around landing on fruit in a bowl on the counter. Now, a single particle of flour might not be enough to cause issues, but flour particles are seldom found alone. How much is too much?

Do you reuse your deep fryer oil? Even filtering oil after use can leave a residue. Heat does NOT kill gluten. Fresh-cut, unseasoned french fries/chips don't have gluten, but if they are fried in oil that also fries onion rings or chicken nuggets that are coated in a gluteny batter, then the oil is cross-contaminated and can make a gluten-intolerant person sick.

HIDDEN GLUTEN

So you stick to fresh fruit and vegetables. They're safe? Maybe just serve candy, because that's just sugar? Or meats - maybe just offer a hot dog or hamburger without a bun? Is meat OK? Or maybe open a can of condensed tomato soup? It's just tomatoes, right?

As gluten is a protein naturally occurring in certain foods you just avoid these foods correct? Unfortunately, though, it can also be added to foods during processing for texture or to thicken gravies, sauces, and soups. It is also often used as a binding agent and flavoring, so you can sometimes find it in foods you wouldn't expect.

Some people think going gluten-free means not eating any carbohydrates, but this isn't the case. There are lots of gluten-free carbohydrates such as rice, potatoes, pulses and legumes (i.e. lentils and beans).

Here are some everyday items that you may be surprised to learn can contain gluten. It **doesn't mean they always do, but they can contain gluten**.

- Normal **Beer**, ale, and lagers.
- **Bouillon** cubes, broth, stocks and concentrated bouillon powder
- **Candy, Sweets and Chocolate/Candy Bars** - Did you know most licorice contains wheat flour? Chocolate bars often contain barley malt and other gluten sources. Both of these sweets and many others sweets, may be subject to cross-contact with gluten during production.
- **Potato chips/Crisps** - Potatoes themselves are gluten-free, but if cooked in a shared oil or added flavors/seasonings can make them unsafe.
- **Nuts -** although nuts are gluten-free, they are often subject to cross-contact issues.
- **Coffee Additive/Creamers** - it's not just dried cream or milk anymore. Many have gluten added.
- **Blue Cheese**
- **Cold cuts, Bologna, Bacon, hot dogs, salami, and sausages.** Even premade meatballs and hamburgers can often contain flour or bread crumbs as a filler or binding agent.
- **French fries/Hot chips** - another gluten-free food that is made unsafe by cooking in contaminated oil or seasoning added.
- **Gravies**
- Imitation fish like **imitation crab** often contains gluten.
- **Rice mixes**. Again rice itself is gluten-free but added flavorings can make it unsafe.
- **Salad Dressings**
- **Sauces and Dips**
- **Seasoned or multigrain tortilla chips**
- **Self-basting turkey**
- **Soups** - Obviously most noodle soups have gluten, but also most cream soups are thickened with flour. In addition, most Condensed soups also contain gluten. For example, Condensed Tomato soup often has wheat flour within the first 5 ingredients.
- **Soy sauce**
- **Vegetables in sauce**
- **Worcestershire Sauce**

WHAT IS CROSS-CONTACT?

Cross-contact is when a food allergen passes to another food. In this case, a non-gluten food item is exposed to a gluten-containing ingredient – making it unsafe for people with a gluten intolerance to eat. There are many obvious (and not-so-obvious) sources of potential cross-contact at home and in restaurants and other food service locations.

There is even a risk of cross-contact before ingredients make it to the kitchen, such as during the growing and manufacturing processes. Grains are a field crop and many farms harvesting these crops grow more than one type. Cross-contact can start right in the field itself. Farmers who grow wheat (which contains gluten) and oats (which is gluten-free) might use the same machinery for both crops. Sometimes, this can cause one product to mingle with the other, either during harvest, transport or while being milled into flour. Suddenly, those gluten-free oats are no longer gluten-free. This same example can apply to products made from corn like corn flour and cornmeal.

As mentioned on previous pages, gluten is tiny and can be transferred easily. Although you can wash gluten from a smooth surface with soap and water, it is a common misconception that boiling water, high heat from an oven or oil in a fryer or even using a cleaning spray will "sanitize" things. However, gluten cannot be "killed off" or "disinfected" like this.

Please note that cross-contact is more often known as cross-contamination and many people in the celiac community often mistakenly use this term. To be fair, cross-contact is a newer term, so some have gotten into the habit of labeling everything involving cross-contact as cross-contamination.

Cross-contamination, however, occurs when a bacteria is transferred from one food product to another. The key mark of distinction is that cross-contamination refers to food-borne bacteria or virus and not food allergens.

Many companies produce both gluten products and gluten-free products. Often these are produced in separate facilities or on separate machines, but not always. Since gluten is so small, it can easily sit in a crevice of a machine that is cleaned regularly. This now is a contaminated piece of machinery. If a gluten-free cracker is now produced on this same machine, this can make a gluten-free cracker unsafe. Usually, this is where the 'May Contain' statement appears.

While it may seem like a challenge to remember and be proactive about all of the possible sources of cross-contact at first, there are ways to make it safer.

CROSS-CONTACT IN YOUR HOME!

Cross-contact can be a huge factor for a gluten-intolerant person, but is normally less important to someone avoiding gluten by choice. Although you're trying to respect their wishes for gluten avoidance, if a crumb of gluten gets through to your food item, they will likely not even realize it was there. On the other hand, most gluten-intolerant people will know if they got glutened from cross-contact, even if it is just a tiny crumb.

These are common areas of the typical home that can contain gluten residue:

Toasters
Colanders/Strainers
Margarine/Butter Dish
Convection Ovens/Air Fryers
Flour sifters
Sponges, Dishcloths
Utensils, Can openers
Pots, pans and skillets with scratches or seams where 2 pieces meet
BBQ Grills and griddles especially cast iron due to textured surface
Deep Fryers containing oil
Cutting boards
Shelves in your refrigerator and pantry
Food Processors/Blenders

As mentioned, gluten cannot be sanitized away, so any gluten that remains on sponges/dishcloths can be transferred to otherwise clean plates and countertops.

Utensils that are used to spread butter, peanut butter, jam, mayonnaise, and other condiments will expose the product to gluten in two ways. Firstly, if the same knife is used to spread a gluten piece of bread and then a gluten-free piece of bread, crumbs could transfer from one to the other quite easily. Secondly, if the spreader goes back into the container to get more, then they risk leaving crumbs in your container for the next person. These crumbs can be pushed a long way into the jar.

Stainless steel pots and pans can usually be scrubbed well with soap and water, but if there are any large scratches in a Non-Stick frypan, gluten can hide in these spots and not be washed away.

Most backyard BBQ grills have seen their share of buns being toasted (or burnt). Just like a toaster, crumbs can reside on the grill and be transferred to a gluten-free bun or steak.

Convection ovens and Air fryers use a fan to circulate air around food. This process can cause cross-contact because gluten particles can be blown by the fan.

It is not safe to use the same oil to fry both gluten and non-gluten items. High heat will not eliminate gluten in the oil, so fryers used to make breaded or battered items would not be safe to use for gluten-free french fries/chips, corn tortilla chips, or other gluten-free items.

Knives can cause cuts on the surface of cutting boards and these are hard to clean out completely. If a cutting board is used to slice, cut or dice gluten-containing items – like bread or dough – gluten can get stuck in these crevices and transfer the gluten to your food. This is more common with wooden cutting boards.

Do you place bread in your brown sugar container to keep it soft? Or maybe in your spice jar to suck up moisture? Or use a piece of bread to clean up coffee grounds or spices from the grinder? Guess what? They are no longer safe!

Although not the most common source of gluten, the refrigerator door handle can contain sticky gluten residue. For example, Mom was preparing cookie/biscuits or has flour-dusted hands and suddenly realizes she's missing an important ingredient. She hastily wipes her hands on the dish towel or apron (which are now also sources of unwanted gluten!) and opens the fridge. Any residual gluten that was on their hands is now on the refrigerator door handle and may be a source of cross-contact later on.

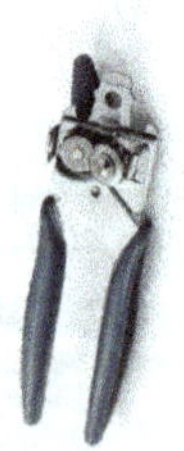

Do you open cans of soup or canned pasta with your can opener?   These products can have gluten and some can leak up over the rim when opened with a can opener. Do you always clean your can opener after use? Whether it's a mounted, hand, or electric can opener, gluten can go up under the metal blade part into harder-to-reach areas waiting for the next can you open.

Most people will be surprised to know that flour can stay airborne for up to 48 hours, depending on ventilation and quantity of flour. While simply touching gluten will not harm an individual with celiac disease, there can be a risk of ingesting airborne gluten, which is usually caused by flour landing on something safe, like fruit. It is also important to remember not to prepare gluten-free foods in spaces where there is a risk of airborne gluten, as particles will settle on the food, making it unsafe for those with celiac disease to eat. Some of the most common places where this type of cross-contact can occur include pizzerias and bakeries.

ORDERING OUT

The previous chapter discussed many places where gluten can reside in your home. Maybe you decide it's too risky to cook at home and you'll just order take-out/take-away instead, right? You see lots of burger and sandwich places offering gluten-free buns and pizza places offering gluten-free pizza crusts all the time!

Restaurants and Fast Food places that aren't 100% gluten-free will experience the same hazards as your home.   Most restaurants will have a separate section in their kitchen to reduce the chances of contamination, but there is always a risk.

Fast Food Restaurants

It's awesome that places are offering choices for people avoiding gluten, however, unless these same places can educate their staff and provide a safer process, then these places are at high risk.

Therefore, it doesn't matter if you're thinking about Subs, Sandwiches, Burgers, Chicken, or maybe Mexican take-out/take-away - a person that has been avoiding gluten for a while knows the questions to ask and usually what they can safely eat, but you likely do NOT. For someone without the background of what to ask, I would suggest you avoid fast food unless you can ask your gluten-free guest what they normally get from a specific place.

Other Restaurants offering Take-out/Take-away

Many sit-down restaurants offer a gluten-free menu and/or gluten-free choices. However once again, only a 100% gluten-free establishment can be truly safe.

You will notice in almost every restaurant that **GF stands for Gluten Friendly, not Gluten Free.** That means they are using gluten-free items, but they are cooked in an area where cross-contact can occur. Staff is normally educated on proper procedures, but staff can rotate and it's human nature to make mistakes when it's busy. I think if you can confirm that the gluten-free food is prepared in a separate area of the kitchen you are doing the best you can. Once again, just communicate the research that you did to your guest.

As always, there are gluten-free people that refuse to eat from a non 100% gluten-free facility, please do not feel their concerns are not authentic. It is always a good idea to ask your guest if they can recommend a safer place to get some food.

There are indeed lots of places offering gluten-free pizza right now. However, many of these chain pizza places state right on their websites that gluten-free pizzas are not recommended for celiacs. Many times the people working at these places are young and inexperienced especially when it comes to cross-contact and how dangerous it can be for gluten to be transferred.

It's great that they have a gluten-free crust option, but it's so easy to transfer a crumb from a regular pizza crust to a gluten-free crust. As Pizza is one of those items that many gluten intolerant will take the risk of, I will discuss this more on the next page.

ORDERING PIZZA

Here is an example of the information taken from one of the major pizza chains in the US and Canada. I have intentionally removed the name of company and also highlighted an important section but I have NOT changed anything else.

Gluten-Smart

CRUST
Although we are confident that this product does not contain gluten, the nature of our open concept kitchens and with dough made fresh daily, present possible flour cross-contamination and therefore gluten exposure.

Subsequently, **this crust is NOT recommended for celiac disease sufferers or those customers with a moderate to high gluten intolerance or sensitivity.**

This crust is free of all major allergens (dairy, eggs, soy, wheat/gluten, sulphite, shellfish, fish, peanuts, tree nuts, mustard seed & sesame seed).

XXXXXXXXX takes food safety and handling very seriously. Our restaurant staff receive a high level of training and there are several procedures in place to keep the potential for cross-contamination at a minimum.

Here is a list of procedures in place to minimize cross-contamination:

• Special square screens have been provided to each store for cooking purposes of this organic gluten-smart crust only
• Clean knives are used for cutting this crust
• Cooking screens are kept in a sealed container when not being used
• Our organic gluten-smart crusts are kept in individually sealed packages and are not opened until the pizza is ordered
• The crust is square to be easily identifiable to all store staff
• Small stickers are adhered to all gluten-smart pizzas that leave the store to emphasize a potential risk to customers who may have gluten intolerances

Pizza continued.......

The **BEST** option is to find a 100% gluten-free pizza place. These places do exist.

The **SECOND** best option is to ask your guest if they can recommend a pizza place they trust?

However, 100% gluten-free places are not always convenient and maybe you want to surprise your guest or you can't contact them. So what's the next best choice?

Lastly, more and more typical pizza chains are jumping on the bandwagon to offer a gluten-free crust. As seen on the previous page, even though it states 'not recommended' for celiacs, it seems with the gluten-free trend that some are offering extra precautions to make it safer. Even though there are always risks, many gluten-intolerant people will take the risk.   Just remember, there is still a chance of cross-contact.

Assuming it isn't a 100% gluten-free pizza place, I would suggest you still request they be extra careful as the pizza is for someone with an 'allergy to gluten'. NO, it's not really an allergy, but it is more commonly understood as serious to state it's an allergy.

If you cannot find any information online, please ask:
A) Is the gluten-free dough made in-house? - If it is, you want to know if they have a dedicated area in the kitchen where the gluten-free dough is prepared or stored to prevent cross-contact. Remember, regular pizza dough made in-house usually means there is flour in the air which can float for up to 48 hours. It is also better if the gluten-free dough is made before the regular dough. This doesn't eliminate the risk, but it does help to reduce it.

OR

B) Is the gluten-free dough made elsewhere and just brought into the store? - If this is the case, you just want to know it's stored safely from the regular dough.

OR

C) Maybe it's a premade gluten-free crust rather than dough? - Then you just want to ensure it is stored safely away from regular pizza dough or crusts.

If the <u>gluten-free dough is made in the same area as regular pizzas</u>, I would avoid this place.

After asking your previous questions and the pizza dough is
deemed safe you can proceed to the next questions. You want
'Yes' to all these questions.

- Is the gluten-free pizza cooked on a separate tray to prevent stray crumbs in the pizza oven while baking?

- Are all the toppings gluten-free? If the pizza place is offering a gluten-free crust they usually know what toppings are safe, but please be aware toppings like Pepperoni and sausage may contain gluten.

- Are the toppings in a closed container or sitting open? Does the person making pizza use their hands/gloves to grab toppings? It is easy for crumbs from a regular pizza to transfer from a glove to a container with toppings. I would request a new pair of gloves be used and they take ingredients from a new container.

- Is the gluten-free pizza cut with a separate or cleaned pizza cutter? If the previous pizza was a regular pizza crust then it can easily leave crumbs on the cutter which can then transfer to the gluten-free pizza. Maybe ask them to ensure it is cleaned or ask for it to not be cut at all and slice it at home.

- Is the pizza sauce spread on the gluten-free pizza using a separate spoon/ladle from a separate sauce container? If the same ladle/spoon is used to put sauce on regular pizza from a common container, the previous regular pizza could have left gluten residue on the ladle which has then contaminated the sauce.

I do believe Pizza is one of those food items that many gluten-intolerant people take a chance on more than others. However, as usual, others won't take the chance on a non-100 % dedicated facility. No one likes to ask so many questions and chances are a gluten-intolerant person would take a risk and not worry about something like the sauce, but you may not know this person. I suggest you err on the side of caution and ask the questions. I think if you have done the research I have highlighted above and then communicated this to your guest, they will appreciate your research.

IT'S HARD!

Maybe you should just give up. It's safer! Right??

I want to state clearly that it **MAY** be possible to prepare an entirely safe meal just by avoiding gluten in your ingredients. Cross-contact doesn't mean it will happen, but it **CAN** and **DOES** happen. Just because your toaster has gluten crumbs, doesn't mean it will transfer to a gluten-free waffle. Not washing a dish, doesn't mean your gluten-free guest will be sick. **HOWEVER**, each thing I mentioned **IS** a potential problem and as we discussed, it doesn't take much to make a gluten-intolerant person sick.

As stated before, don't be upset if you meet people with celiac disease that refuse to eat anything you prepare, no matter how safe you make it. No matter how careful you are, there can always be a risk. Please don't think it's not as dangerous as an allergy. Yes, indeed, most celiacs will not die immediately from eating something with gluten like an anaphylactic reaction. But as a Mom that has watched her young daughter fall asleep on the bathroom floor because she refuses to let go of the toilet seat due to dry heaving for hours, you don't like to take chances. I have heard lots of stories of people having to go to the hospital as they are unable to function after a full day of vomiting or just the severity of their reactions. Many do not take that chance and it is perfectly acceptable for them to do so.

However, if there were NO gluten-intolerant people willing to eat out, I wouldn't be creating this cookbook. I do believe that most gluten avoiders will eat out if they feel the host understands the steps that are needed to make it safe.

My intention with this book is to provide tips and suggestions on how to make it as safe as possible using simple ingredients you can easily find at most grocery stores. Whether you prepare it at home or order take-out, many celiacs will eat options if they know it was prepared safely. It is always best to share your steps with your guest to help them feel comfortable.

GENERAL TIPS

The following are simple ideas to help you avoid cross-contact in your home.

- **Always use parchment paper** or aluminum/aluminium foil on cooking sheets and pans to prevent cross-contact when baking in the oven and foil for the BBQ or on the grill.

- If your oven is a **convection oven** or you like to use an **air fryer**, please only use a regular oven setting instead. It may take longer to cook, but convection ovens and air fryers have circulating fans to move air around which can also recirculate gluten.

- If you don't have a non-convection setting, you can still use a convection oven that has been used to prepare gluten-containing foods, but only as long as you keep gluten-free foods tightly covered when cooking. For example, using aluminum foil.

- Avoid using any **porous containers**, bowls, or cookware that isn't sealed with some sort of coating. Gluten can hide on porous surfaces. It is safer to use stainless steel, glass, or anything smooth-sided that can be washed clean before use.

- Any **kitchen utensil** that has ridges or seams between two pieces like where a handle attaches to the pot and where gluten can hide should be cleaned before use. Rivets can also hide gluten.

- Any item made of **wood** like spoons, rolling pins, spatulas, and cutting boards, is just too hard to clean and should not be used.

- If your **spatula** has a removable head from the base, please avoid using it. Gluten can easily be hiding in the tip which is hard to clean efficiently. One piece, silicon or plastic is best.

- **Toaster ovens** are acceptable to use too, and using foil or a clean tray on the rack helps create a barrier from any crumbs. Also, be sure to thoroughly clean the oven in between uses, even if there are no visible crumbs.

- **Toasters** are often a source of cross-contact. Think about all those crumbs in the one sitting on your counter right now! You can, however, purchase something called a "toaster bag". These are bread sized, parchment-like reusable bags that allow you to put something in your toaster, but still protect it from cross-contact. These can be found online or sometimes at a department or grocery store.

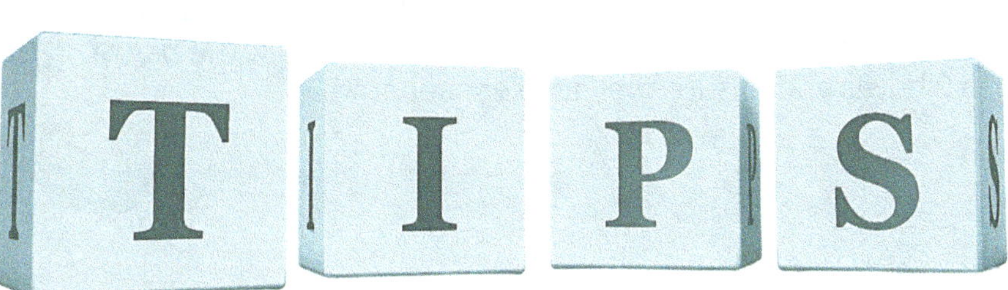

Tips continued........

- Always use a **clean cloth or sponge** for cleaning in the kitchen before cooking gluten-free. Gluten can easily reside within a cloth and transfer back to a kitchen counter or pot when you are trying to actually clean it.

- Even if all dishes are gluten-free, **ensure each bowl always has its own spoon** or serving utensil Maybe also state to ALL guests how important it is to not mix these spoons up. It's essential if there are gluten items at the table, but just good practice in general.

- **Cooling racks** can have too many joins to be safe for use directly with food. I suggest cleaning it well with soap and water and then covering it before use with a clean, cotton towel, paper towel, or parchment paper. You want something that will still allow air to circulate without the food coming in contact with the metal itself.

- **Colanders and strainers** are notoriously difficult to clean. They just have too many places to hold gluten. If you need to strain something, I suggest holding the clean lid over the pot with a slight opening for the water to drain out. The trick is to make sure the opening for the lid is smaller than the size of your item and to pour slowly. If you are not comfortable doing this, I suggest cleaning the colander well with soap and water and then similar to the cooling rack above, place a clean, cotton dishtowel over the colander or strainer and then pour it into the dishtowel to keep the food item from contacting the colander. Then carefully lift the hot towel allowing water to drip and then place food into a bowl.

- Carefully watch your jarred or container **condiments**. Double dipping into butter/margarine or other condiments is dangerous. It's always best to have a clearly marked gluten-free version of your condiments. A piece of masking tape and a pen is all you need to identify it clearly. Even if you have a separate dish for gluten-free people, it's a good habit to suggest to others to just take a scoop of butter and place it on your plate and then use this to spread your bread rather than re-scooping with a dirty utensil.

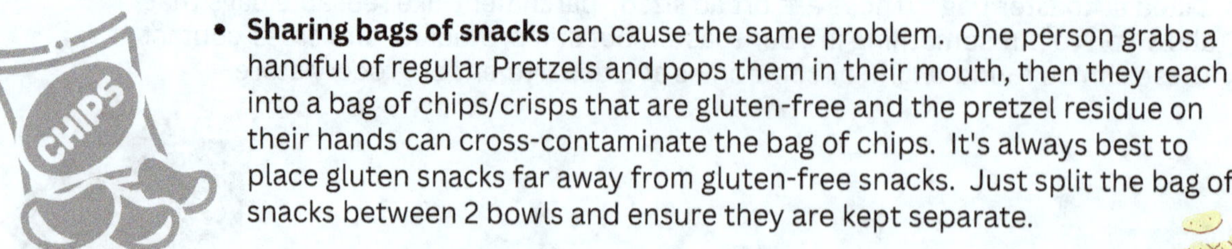

- If you do have gluten and non-gluten items available to **dip**, please don't create an environment where you can dip a gluten item into a non-gluten product. Just a single dip of a gluten item can contaminate the dip for any person avoiding gluten. It's best to include 2 dips or at least 2 bowls of the same dip, separated if possible. Try to have gluten-free dipping items around one dip and gluten items around the other. Maybe advise guests to ensure they don't dip into the wrong dip.

- **Sharing bags of snacks** can cause the same problem. One person grabs a handful of regular Pretzels and pops them in their mouth, then they reach into a bag of chips/crisps that are gluten-free and the pretzel residue on their hands can cross-contaminate the bag of chips. It's always best to place gluten snacks far away from gluten-free snacks. Just split the bag of snacks between 2 bowls and ensure they are kept separate.

- Although there is still a risk for cross-contact, you may find using **condiments in squeeze bottles** more useful as long as those using the condiments are well aware that they cannot wipe the tip of the squirt bottle on their gluten-containing foods. If you are not 100% sure your squeeze bottle hasn't been wiped on a piece of bread, please only use a new bottle.

- Although making things from scratch is usually preferred, when you're occasionally making gluten-free items in an area that's not normally gluten-free, it is safer to use a **pre-packaged mix** than measuring different flours, salt, baking soda, etc. Cake mixes, biscuits, quick breads, cookies and other items can be found pre-packaged and are usually found along side regular mixes.

- If you are using a **cooking spray** to grease your pan please ensure it is gluten-free as well. Most regular sprays do not have gluten, but there are a few ones that are meant for baking and include flour to prevent sticking. Avoid using these.

- If the **BBQ grill** has been exposed to gluten, heavy, sturdy foil can be put on the grill or a sauté pan should be used instead.

- Try to avoid using used **plastic containers** that may have contained a gluten source. Disposable plastic/tupperware containers are fairly cheap and much safer if new. If you have no other option, inspect your containers carefully for scratches, and assuming none, carefully wash the container ensuring you get under the lid and corners.

- If possible, it is always better to **use fresh meat, fish, fruit, and vegetables**. Simple eggs and cheese are easy to use. As well as base ingredients like rice, corn, soy and potato products.

- **Spices** are used a lot in all types of cooking but many are processed in facilities where gluten exists. Although they don't 'contain' gluten, please watch for 'may contain' statements on ALL your spices.

- Make sure to regularly clean your **refrigerator door** and other handles in the kitchen to ensure that you don't accidentally transfer gluten when you're grabbing a quick bite to eat from the fridge

- Keep gluten-containing food away from the meal you are preparing.

- Keep gluten-containing dishes away from finished gluten-free dishes. I would even suggest you place a note on gluten-free dishes so non-gluten-free people are aware to take more care. Even seasoned gluten-avoiders can easily grab the wrong item.

39

- Be careful of **cutlery or serving ware** found in your drawers. A silverware divider in your drawer always seems to become an eerie collection of all things crumbs. Please wash anything from this drawer before using or setting the table.

- Make sure to also **use fresh dishwater** if you hand wash your dishes, as particles of gluten in the water can also be transferred to otherwise clean dishes when rinsing. Save dishes that held gluten-containing foods for last when hand-washing dishes.

- If you use a **food processor or blender** for anything, please make sure you clean it well including running the blender with water and a few drops of dish soap to better clean where the blades turn. These are hard areas to clean and could hide residual gluten from a previous food item.

- Not normally a high source for cross-contact, but please carefully wipe the cutting edge on your **can opener**. If the last thing you opened contained gluten, then this can contaminate the current cans you need to open.

  - **Stand or Hand Mixers** - Unfortunately, it is really hard to clean some of the areas on these machines. With moving parts there is always potential for gluten to hide where you can't clean, like where the beaters attach. The safest way to whip or mix anything is by hand, but sometimes it is just unrealistic to do this. If you do decide to use your mixer, please ensure that the entire mixer, beaters, and/or whisk attachment are clean including the area where they attach to the unit. I suggest using a small brush to get in where it is hard to just wipe and is easy for gluten to hide like the holes where the beaters go and the tiny spaces of the whisk where it comes together at the top and bottom. Do NOT bang the beaters or whisk attachment on the mixer bowl as this may dislodge flour particles that remain in areas that are hard to clean.

ALWAYS READ LABELS. Even if something has always been gluten-free in the past or maybe online it states it is gluten-free. The only final place to check ingredients is the label on the product itself.

Recipes

The following recipes aren't meant to be revolutionary. Although I have tried to select appetizing recipes, my main focus is how to cook for a gluten-intolerant person safely on an <u>occasional basis</u>.

If you are switching your style to cook gluten-free all the time or maybe you are switching your entire home over to be gluten-free only, then this cookbook may still benefit you, but that was not my focus.

If you are looking for more unique or unusual recipes and are willing to do more intense shopping, you can search the internet and then apply my suggestions on how to make it safe in your non gluten-free home.

The recipes all state, how many Servings, Prep Time, Cook Time, and Ease of preparation. Please note that Prep time includes all active time to get the dish ready. This will include mixing, stirring, mashing, and other steps in the recipe's instructions including any active cooking like sautéing and frying. It does not include any marinating or refrigeration time, but this should be noted under prep time or cook time.

I also realize that many gluten-intolerant people also have other intolerances and allergies such as dairy, eggs, etc. While not all of my recipes specifically state replacement options, I have simply replaced some items, like using a lactose-free version of cream cheese, with no issues. Since these recipes were all chosen for ease of preparation, aside from ones that rely heavily on that allergen, like an egg dish, I feel confident stating that you can just replace the allergen with your choice of a suitable substitute. Recipes like my version of a Frittata, would likely require finding a new recipe, but you can still use my suggestions and tips to make a suitable safe version.

RECIPES

Specifically, the recipes were chosen for a few reasons:

Firstly, they are all tried and true favorites. Although I can't possibly predict what all others will like, these are recipes that have been around for a while or have been served to many people, both people who do not consume gluten and those that do, successfully.

Secondly, they are easy to prepare for both seasoned chefs and those more cooking challenged. Many only have a few ingredients and a few steps. Some of the recipes, like for potatoes and vegetables, are more just suggestions on how to make them safe for gluten-intolerant people.

Third, most don't contain any hard-to-find ingredients. Gluten-free baking usually involves a combination of various gluten-free flours (Rice, Corn, Tapioca Starch, etc.) and additives to mimic the missing gluten which normally "glues" the product together. I don't expect you to shop for 3 different flours or Psyllium Husk or Xanthan Gum. For this reason, I've tried to select recipes that use pre-packaged mixes or limited unusual ingredients. These are much easier to find and use.

And lastly, recipes were chosen so you can easily take steps to make them safer from cross-contact. Opening a box, for example, is easier than buying, sorting, and cooking an item. There is always a risk, but if we can limit the number of risks within each recipe, the results will be safer for your gluten-free guest.

I apologize if you need nutritional information for these recipes. All my chosen recipes were taken from my recipe library and some were taken from internet sites a long time ago which I adapted to make gluten-free. Some were just written down by my Mom, many years ago and converted to be gluten-free. I no longer have or keep the nutritional information and I don't think most people even use them. If you are someone that does use this information, there are LOADS of free resources on the internet that will allow you to calculate the nutritional facts of any recipe – on demand, in only a few minutes.

BREAKFAST

Breakfast is known as the most important meal of the day! It's your chance to have or provide a healthy, nourishing meal that will give everyone enough energy to get through the day. Just because you need to avoid gluten, doesn't mean it can't be nutritious and most importantly, delicious!

Basic morning food is still a possibility when you are avoiding gluten. There's nothing like a bowl of warm oatmeal/porridge, a sweet bowl of cereal, scrambled eggs, or even pancakes or waffles.   You just need to be aware or know where to look and what to avoid.

Let's start with the easy things - There are some wonderful certified gluten-free **cereals** to enjoy. These will vary by country. Some you can even find in your regular cereal aisle, but you can also find more in the Organic/Gluten-Free section of the store. Just be careful if shopping in the Organic/Gluten Free section as there are cereals that are Organic, but not gluten-free. No matter where you shop, just remember to **always read the label** and only choose cereals with a gluten-free claim on the box. In the USA, this should be expanded to avoid ones that do not have certified gluten-free oats or corn. Also, consider **Granola** and **Oatmeal** to be part of this option. There are some wonderful granolas available, but due to the same chances of cross-contact, these need to state gluten-free.

Check your fridge for **yogurt**. Although there are some flavors and brands that may contain gluten, there are lots of delicious options. Let's not forgot the basic fresh **fruit** option. Even kids enjoy fruit.

Eggs are naturally gluten-free so feel free to cook these up in any style you wish in a clean pan - fried, poached, or scrambled. Just watch any additives and as usual, cross-contact with butter and spices. Also, pair it with the classic **bacon**. It's a strange thought for some, but wheat can be added as a binder in some bacon. You can usually easily find the safe ones.

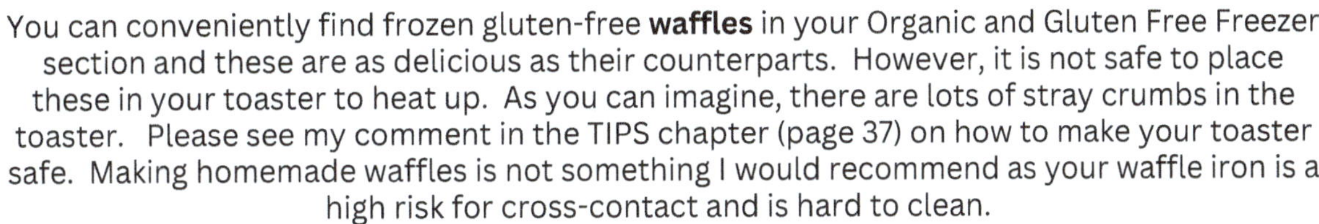

You can conveniently find frozen gluten-free **waffles** in your Organic and Gluten Free Freezer section and these are as delicious as their counterparts. However, it is not safe to place these in your toaster to heat up. As you can imagine, there are lots of stray crumbs in the toaster. Please see my comment in the TIPS chapter (page 37) on how to make your toaster safe. Making homemade waffles is not something I would recommend as your waffle iron is a high risk for cross-contact and is hard to clean.

Pancakes on the other hand are much easier to make gluten-free at home safely. I've yet to find a really bad-tasting gluten-free pancake mix. There are many great options for premade mixes in the Organic or Gluten Free section of your grocery store. Most just add either water or maybe milk, oil, or an egg and they can be fried up in a clean skillet.

HASH BROWN CRUST QUICHE

This gluten-free quiche with a hash brown crust is an easy, healthy, and very filling recipe. It can be made ahead, customized to suit your tastes, and even vegetarian-friendly if you're willing to leave out the bacon!

With loads of protein from eggs and cheese and potentially lots of veggies, this one-dish meal is perfect when you need to make something quick, easy, and tasty.

 **Prep**
20 Mins

 **Cook Time**
60-70 Mins

 **Serves**
8

 **Difficulty**
Easy

Ingredients

Crust

15 oz (425 g) bag of frozen hash browns, thawed OR 8 oz dehydrated (238 g) hash browns OR 4 cups shredded potatoes

1/4 cup (30 g) cheese, shredded

1 tablespoon (15 ml) butter, melted

1 tablespoon (15 ml) olive oil

1/2 teaspoon sea salt

1/4 teaspoon freshly ground black pepper

Filling

6 large eggs

1/2 cup (125 ml) milk

1 tablespoon (15 ml) of your favorite mustard

1/2 teaspoon garlic powder

1/4 teaspoon pepper

4 slices bacon, finely diced

1 small green or red pepper, diced

1/2 cup (15 g) spinach, chopped

1 cup (80 g) cheese, shredded

 Believe and you will achieve.

Special Supplies

- a glass pie plate is best, but you can use a clean aluminum/aluminium pan or an 8" x 8" (20cm x 20cm) pan.

- Gluten-free frozen hash browns can usually be found in the freezer section of your local grocery stores near the frozen french fries/chips. Just watch for special seasonings that may contain gluten or sometimes wheat flour is added. Ensure you check the ingredients label.

- If you can't find gluten-free hash browns, you can just grate your own potatoes. This is a safe option, except for maybe your fingertips so be careful with the grater. You'll need about 4 cups.

- Dehydrated hash browns can be found in most local grocery stores. They are usually just potatoes, but please still check the ingredients label.

Gluten Precautions

- Bacon - Hard to believe, but you need to check the ingredients label of bacon. A surprising number of packages contain gluten.

- Spices are used a lot in all types of cooking, but many are processed in facilities where gluten exists. Although they don't 'contain' gluten, please watch for 'may contain' statements on ALL your spices.

- Carefully wash your grater prior to shredding potatoes and/or cheese. There are lots of tiny hidden areas on a grater so use a brush to get into all tiny areas and openings.

- If you are using a spray to grease your pan please ensure it is gluten-free as well. Most regular sprays do not have gluten, but there are a few that are meant for baking and include flour to prevent sticking. Avoid using these.

- Butter/Margarine is a common source of cross-contact issues. Please be careful to ensure there are no crumb particles.

- Mustard is more commonly found in a squeeze bottle but it is still possible for gluten crumbs to be sucked into the tip when the squeeze is released if the tip is wiped on bread for example. Please buy or open a new bottle if there is any chance of crumbs.

- Colanders and strainers are notoriously hard to clean and should be avoided. If you need to drain your shredded potato after you rinse them, I suggest you check out my Tips chapter on page 38 for suggestions on doing this safely. If you tightly squeeze the dishtowel with the potatoes you can get most of the moisture out.

- Ensure this is cooked in a non-convection oven as we don't want the air circulating while this bakes.

Directions

STEP 1

Preheat your oven to **400°F (200°C)**. Grease/Spray a 9" (23 cm) round pie plate and set aside.

If using **dehydrated** hash browns, rehydrate as instructed on the packaging. If using **fresh potatoes**, please shred them carefully and rinse them with cold water for 30 seconds. Drain and squeeze dry. If using **frozen** hash browns, please ensure they are thawed and then squeezed dry to reduce moisture.

STEP 2

Mix the hash browns, 1/4 cup cheese, butter, olive oil, salt, and pepper. Evenly press the hash brown mixture into the bottom and up the sides of the pan, making sure it is evenly distributed. Pack the crust well. Spray the crust with oil lightly.

STEP 3

Put the prepared pie plate with crust into the preheated oven. Bake for 25-30 minutes until the crust just begins to brown. Continue with next steps while the crust bakes.

STEP 4

Cook the diced bacon in a sauté pan over medium-high heat, stirring occasionally until it just begins to brown. Add the diced bell peppers and cook until soft and the bacon is browned (about 4-5 minutes). Add spinach and turn off the heat to cool slightly.

STEP 5

Whisk together eggs, milk, mustard, garlic powder, and pepper in a large bowl. Add the 1 cup of cheese and stir to combine. Add cooked bacon mixture and stir. Set aside until the crust is done baking.

STEP 6

Once the crust is done, remove it from the oven and reduce the oven temperature to **350°F (177°C)**. Carefully pour the filling into your prepared hash brown crust. Return to the oven and bake at the reduced temperature for 30 minutes or until the filling is set and golden in color. Let it stand for about 10 minutes before serving. Can be served cool too.

Notes

- Please use your creativity to think of new additives or remove ones you don't want. Just ensure anything you add is gluten-free. If you don't like spinach, leave it out. If you want it spicy, throw in some red pepper flakes or hot sauce.
- Store in an airtight container in the refrigerator for up to 5 days, and the freezer for up to 2 months. Reheat in the oven or microwave until warmed through.

CLOUD BREAD

What's that? You've never heard of cloud bread? You're not alone.
Cloud Bread is high in protein and low in carbohydrates, making it a delightful bread for those avoiding gluten.

Its name refers to the texture being light and fluffy. You'll be amazed at how easy it is to make and you may find yourself making this recipe even when your gluten-free guest isn't around.

In this case, I have included it in the breakfast section as although the cloud bread is amazing by itself, I think it works well for an egg sandwich or a BLT sandwich. Or can just be an addition to your egg dish.

 **Prep**
20 Mins

 **Cook Time**
30 Mins

 **Serves**
12

 **Difficulty**
Easy

Ingredients

4 large eggs, separated

1/2 teaspoon cream of tartar

1 teaspoon Italian herb seasoning

1/2 teaspoon sea salt

1/4 teaspoon garlic powder

2 oz (62 g) cream cheese - room temperature

Special Supplies

- parchment paper

Gluten Precautions

- Ensure these are cooked in a non-convection oven as we don't want the air circulating while they bake.

- Using parchment paper will prevent contact with whatever may have been previously made on this same baking sheet. It also makes it easier and safer to remove from the baking sheet.

- The safest way to whip the egg whites is by hand, but this is unrealistic in this case due to the amount of whipping necessary. I suggest you use your stand mixer or hand mixer and the whisk attachment. However, please ensure that the entire mixer and whisk attachment are clean including the area where the whisk attaches to the unit. I suggest using a small brush to get in where it is hard to just wipe and is easy for gluten to hide like the holes where the beaters go and the tiny spaces of the whisk where it comes together at the top and bottom.

- As spices may be processed in facilities where gluten exists, please watch for 'contains' gluten, and 'may contain' statements on ALL your spices.

Directions

STEP 1

Preheat your oven to **300°F (150°C)**. Line two large baking sheets with parchment paper.

STEP 2

If you haven't already done so, separate the egg whites and egg yolks.

Place the egg whites in a clean stand mixer with a whisk attachment or a medium bowl for a hand mixer. Add the cream of tartar and beat on high until the froth turns to really stiff peaks. Set aside or move to a separate bowl.

STEP 3

Place the cream cheese in a medium bowl or the now empty stand mixing bowl. Residual egg white is not a problem. Beat on high to soften the cream cheese. Then add the egg yolks, one at a time to incorporate. Scrape the bowl and beat until the mixture is completely smooth. It really needs to be perfectly smooth. Then beat in the Italian seasoning, salt, and garlic powder.

STEP 4

Gently fold the firm, whipped whites into the yolk mixture. Try not to deflate them as much as possible as you want the mixture as firm and foamy as possible. Spoon 12 equal, approximately 4" (10cm) circles on the baking sheets - 6 per baking sheet. Make sure to leave space around each circle. If you have some batter left over, go back and distribute it evenly among the piles. Perfect, equal-sized circles are only required if making sandwiches as it is nice for top and bottom sizes to match.

STEP 5

Bake for around 20-25 minutes or up to 30 minutes. The bread should be golden on the outside and firm. The center should not jiggle. D not move to the cooling rack. Cool for several minutes on the baking sheets, then remove and serve!

Notes

- This can be stored as is, in an airtight container in the refrigerator for several days. However the texture is best if eaten within 12 hours of baking.
- If making sandwiches, please be aware that wet toppings like tomatoes or mayo will soak into and soften the bread. Therefore sandwiches should only be made right before consuming or the texture of the cloud bread will be affected and it may fall apart.

Naturally gluten-free and very easy to make vegetarian, frittatas are a wonderfully flexible meal.

They come together easily and with just a few ingredients and a pan, you'll get a breakfast worthy of serving guests. I have included it under breakfast, but don't be afraid to make this for any meal.

I can't tell you how many times I have made one of these based mostly on what I find unused or leftover in my fridge. I have included what are the most commonly enjoyed additives, but please feel free to substitute as desired.

 **Prep**
10 Mins

 **Cook Time**
30 Mins

 **Serves**
4

 **Difficulty**
Easy

Ingredients

6 large eggs

1/4 cup (60 ml) milk

1 cup (83 g) grated cheese

2-3 cups (500-750 ml) of any chopped vegetables of your choice - For example onions, tomatoes, bell peppers, spinach, broccoli, asparagus, mushrooms, etc.

1 tablespoon (15 ml) butter

Herbs, optional but basil is ideal

Salt and Pepper to taste

It's all in how you look at things!

Special Supplies

- parchment paper
- a 9"x 9" (23cm x 23cm) baking dish or an oven-safe, non-cast iron pan

Gluten Precautions

- Ensure this is cooked in a non-convection oven. We don't want the air circulating while this bakes.

- If you are using a baking dish, using parchment paper will prevent contact with whatever may have been previously made in this same pan, but also aids in removing this frittata to serve. Please see the Appendix on pages 166 -167 for tips.

- As spices may be processed in facilities where gluten exists, please watch for 'contains' gluten, and 'may contain' statements on ALL your spices.

- If you are using a spray to grease your pan please ensure it is gluten-free as well. Most regular sprays do not have gluten, but there are a few ones that are meant for baking and include flour to prevent sticking. Avoid using these.

- I don't suggest you use a cast iron pan for this dish. Although it is oven safe and holds heat wonderfully, it can also hold gluten and you shouldn't wash cast iron with soap and water or you'll destroy any seasoning you've built up. I would suggest using an oven-safe metal fry pan right from the beginning. If you don't have an oven-safe pan, then use the 9" x 9" pan.

Directions

STEP 1

Preheat the oven to **400°F (200°C)**. If using a 9" (23cm) square baking dish, you should line it with parchment paper.   Please see the Appendix on pages 166 -167 for tips.

STEP 2 - OPTIONAL

I prefer to precook my vegetables, but this is an optional step. To do this just melt a tablespoon (15 ml) of butter in a clean frypan and add vegetables. Fry until slightly soft - about 5 minutes. Set aside to cool slightly.

STEP 3

In a medium bowl, whisk together eggs, cheese, milk, and any herbs and seasonings. If you are using an oven-safe pan, just pour the egg mixture into the pan with the cooked vegetables. Otherwise, add vegetables to this egg mixture then pour the mixture into your baking dish.

STEP 4

Place the egg mixture into the oven. Bake until the frittata is golden and puffy and the center feels firm and springy. This should take about 25 minutes but maybe slightly more.

Notes

- This can be stored in an airtight container in the refrigerator for several days. However, the texture is best if eaten within 12 hours of baking.

- Feel free to add some extra vegetables or cheese just be careful to not add too much as the cooking time will vary too much and you want to ensure the egg cooks through without the edges getting too brown.

SNACKS

Who doesn't enjoy snacks? Whether it's crackers, popcorn, nuts, potato chips/crisps, etc., I'm sure we all have had a time in our lives when we ended up snacking through a meal, rather than making a meal. Although they are not always healthy, they are a bit of indulgence and best of all they provide comfort and are usually easy to prepare or even just grab from a shelf.

Guests don't always provide advance notice. Kids don't always plan very well either. I often get the "We're hungry" unexpectedly when my kid's friends are over. Usually, you can just open your pantry door and grab something. But what happens now if your guest can't have gluten?

In this chapter, we will be looking at snacks to satisfy the cravings of your gluten-free guest. For more options, please also take a look at the School Safe Snacks chapter (page 65) as well!

I loved the Bits & Bites/Nuts & Bolts I had as child. Those little cheese-bit crackers were my favorite. I didn't know about Chex mix until we started eating gluten-free. I liked the original recipe I found, but I missed the cheese aspect I loved as a kid. Therefore I changed it up to meet my taste and ended up with this recipe. That's what I love about this recipe, it is very easy to adapt as required.

Many great kinds of cereals, nuts, and other additives are included and you can easily switch up anything. If you can't find Chex where you live, select another low-sweetness cereal or mix it up another way with crackers, broken-up rice or corn thins/cakes, cheese puffs, nuts, popcorn etc. If you do change it up, keep the same approximate measurements ensuring a correct balance between the seasoning and mix.

NUTS & BOLTS
(AKA CHEX MIX)

 **Prep**
5 Mins

 **Cook Time**
40 Mins

 **Serves**
10 cups

 **Difficulty**
Easy

Ingredients

3 cups (620 ml) rice Chex style cereal

3 cups (620 ml) corn Chex style cereal

2 cups (480 ml) gluten-free pretzels

1/2 cup (120ml) small gluten-free crackers

1/2 cup (120ml) gluten-free 'O' cereal

3/4 cup (180 ml) mixed nuts

3/4 cup (180 ml) cashews

1 cup (250 ml) cheese crisps

8 tablespoons (112 g) butter

2 teaspoons (10 ml) Worcestershire sauce

2 teaspoons (10 ml) seasoned salt

1/2 teaspoon garlic powder

1/2 teaspoon onion powder

Think outside the box.

Special Supplies

- parchment paper

- Cheese crisps are a newer ingredient in today's world. They really are just melted cheese and are found in a variety of flavors in most grocery stores. I like a cheddar flavor, but mix it up. Please see my recipe in the Snack chapter (page 61), to make them yourself.

- Gluten-free pretzels can be found easily in most grocery stores. If not with the regular pretzels, please check your Organic or Gluten Free section of the store.

- There are really good alternate cereals to use but again, all cereals need to state gluten-free or be certified gluten-free in the USA to be safe. I would look in the Organic or Gluten Free aisle for an 'O' Cereal.

- Chex is one of those cereals that are available in the regular cereal aisle in the US and Canada. Any less sweet, gluten-free cereal will work.

Gluten Precautions

- There are lots of ingredients in this recipe that have gluten and gluten-free options. Please be careful and check the ingredient label on everything you choose and all customizable additives.

- Even though you will need to ensure your pan is clean, please still use parchment paper. It is much easier to deal with the cooled mix using parchment paper.

- Nuts themselves are gluten-free and can be found easily in most grocery stores, but you will have to watch for 'May Contain' warnings. Many are processed in a facility with wheat and are therefore not safe to use.

- Ensure this is cooked in a non-convection oven as we don't want the air circulating while this bakes.

- Butter/Margarine is a common source of cross-contact issues. Please be careful to ensure there are no crumb particles.

- Spices are used a lot in all types of cooking, but many are processed in facilities where gluten exists. Although they don't 'contain' gluten, please watch for 'may contain' statements on ALL your spices.

- Worcestershire sauce is often a hidden gluten item. Please carefully verify this is gluten-free and select different brands if necessary. It does provide a great flavor, but if you cannot find a gluten-free version, just leave it out.

Directions

STEP 1

Preheat your oven to **300°F (150°C)**. Cover a baking sheet with parchment paper and set aside.

STEP 2

Place cereals, crackers, nuts and pretzels into a large bowl. Do not include the cheese crisps at this time. Set aside.

Melt the butter in a microwave-safe bowl. To the butter add the Worcestershire sauce, seasonings, and spices and whisk until well combined. Be careful with the seasoning salt as many of your ingredients already are salted.

STEP 3

Pour the butter mixture over the cereal mixture and mix until well coated. Pour on a baking sheet and spread evenly. Bake for 30 to 40 minutes stirring halfway through baking. Remove from oven. Add cheese crisps at this point and stir. Allow to cool.

Notes

- You can mix up the cereal too. As long as the cereal is certified gluten-free, feel free to use another cereal that is not overly sweet.

- You can add new toppings as well - I sometimes add popcorn or in Canada, they have Hickory sticks (small, skinny, hickory-smoke flavored potato sticks) that are awesome in these but if you are adding anything new, make sure you stick to around 8-10 cups total to have the same seasoning to mix ratio.

I saw this recipe one day when I wanted to make Muddy Buddies (a chocolate version of this dish) However, this recipe provided a different taste combination which to me was unique. I love lemons and it seemed lighter, although I don't think it really is. I still like the chocolate version, but if you are looking for something a little different try this recipe. Once again, it lists a Chex-type cereal but for those that cannot access Chex, I would suggest a cornflake or 'O' type of gluten-free cereal.

Just be aware though, this recipe uses white baking chips NOT white chocolate and it doesn't work if you use white chocolate.

This is a nice snack. It's not too sweet and the light citrus taste is delightful. Very simple to put together.

LEMON SNACK MIX

 **Prep**
15 Mins

 **Cook Time**
None

 **Serves**
10 cups

 **Difficulty**
Easy

Ingredients

5 cups (1250 ml) Rice Chex

4 cups (1000 ml) Corn Chex

1-1/2 cups (375 ml) white baking chips (NOT WHITE CHOCOLATE)

4 teaspoons (20 ml) grated lemon zest

2 tablespoons (30 ml) lemon juice

1/4 cup (56 g) butter, softened

1-1/2 cups (375 ml or 168 g) confectioners' sugar (aka powdered/icing sugar)

Special Supplies

- parchment paper
- Double boiler, Microwave or see Notes for alternate method.
- White baking chips are usually found near the regular chocolate chips at your local grocery store. However, you do want baking chips which should not have cocoa butter like white chocolate chips and instead will have a more refined fat which will make them much more forgiving when melted.
- Chex is one of those cereals that is available in the regular cereal aisle in Canada and the USA. However, any of the same types of rice or corn cereals would be great too, or as suggested a corn flake or 'O' type cereal will work as well. Just ensure it is labeled gluten-free.

Gluten Precautions

- Even though you will need to ensure your pan is clean, please still use parchment paper. It is much easier to deal with the cooled mix using parchment paper.
- Butter/Margarine is a common source of cross-contact issues. Please be careful to ensure there are no crumb particles.

Directions

STEP 1

Place cereals into a large bowl. Set aside.

STEP 2

In the top of a clean double boiler melt baking chips with the lemon zest and juice. Stir frequently until smooth.   Stir in butter until blended. **OR** Microwave the baking chips, lemon zest, and juice, uncovered, on high for 1 minute, then stir. Continue warming mixture in small increments until smooth and combined, about 30 seconds longer. Add butter to the warm mixture and continue to stir until completely smooth.

STEP 3

Pour over cereal and toss to coat. If using a smaller or more delicate flaked cereal, stir carefully to avoid crushing it. Sprinkle the confectioners' sugar on top and toss to coat. Spread onto parchment paper to cool. You can store it in an airtight container.

Notes

- This is easiest to make using your microwave. If you don't have a microwave or a double boiler, just place a small pot with a little water on the stove on low heat. Find a glass or metal bowl that fits over the pot but doesn't touch the water. You want indirect heat.
- You will likely need 2 lemons for the zest but you only will need 1 lemon for the juice.
  - You can mix up the cereal too. There is a blueberry Chex that would be a perfect match for the lemon.

We eat A LOT of popcorn, I mean really A LOT. It can be prepared in many ways, it's economical and easy to find. It can even be purchased in premade bags. It is delicious and healthy, well at least before you add toppings.

This is one of our favorite toppings. Nothing wrong with just salt and butter, but this is such a unique flavor combination it is our usual go-to.

 **Prep**
5 Mins

 **Cook Time**
None

 **Serves**
2-3

 **Difficulty**
Easy

Ingredients

10 cups (80 g) popped popcorn, about 1/3-1/2 cup (80 - 100 g) kernels

1/4 cup (57 g) butter, melted

1/4 cup (15 g) nutritional yeast

1 teaspoon salt

1 teaspoon ground paprika

1/2 teaspoon garlic powder

1/2 teaspoon onion powder

1/2 teaspoon chili powder

1/4 teaspoon ground cumin

1/8 teaspoon ground cayenne pepper

NACHO POPCORN

Aim high, dream bigger.

Special Supplies

- Nutritional yeast can usually be found in your local grocery store in the Organic or Gluten Free section of the store. If you can't find it, you can substitute it with 1/4 cup (23 g) of parmesan cheese (the shaker stuff is better than fresh in this case).

Gluten Precautions

- If your popcorn isn't popped, just pop as you normally would. Typically, a regular-sized bag of microwave popcorn will make approximately 4 1/2 cups popped. If you are using a pre-packaged microwave bag, cook as per the instructions on the bag. I have never seen any packaged PLAIN popcorn that isn't gluten-free. Just ensure you check the package's ingredient label for gluten.
- Spices are used a lot in all types of cooking, but many are processed in facilities where gluten exists. Although they don't 'contain' gluten, please watch for 'may contain' statements on ALL your spices.
- Butter/Margarine is a common source of cross-contact issues. Please be careful to ensure there are no crumb particles.

Directions

STEP 1

Mix dry seasoning ingredients in a small bowl. Set aside.

STEP 2

Pop the popcorn, if needed, and then place popped corn into a large bowl. Add any butter or margarine and then sprinkle the seasoning on top. Enjoy!

Notes

- I do 4 or 5 times the dry seasoning mix and just keep it in a sealed container for easy use.

- If you do use parmesan cheese in place of nutritional yeast, I would suggest using the shakers of parmesan rather than fresh grated. The shakers are drier and it sticks better. Just verify ingredients as gluten-free on the shaker.

CHEESE CRISPS

Cheese crisps gained a lot of popularity with low-carb and gluten-free diets becoming popular.   They are delicious as a snack and can be used as a salad topper, or on a sandwich. I like to also use these in my Nuts and Bolts and trail mixes.

You can buy these easily nowadays, but they are very simple to make on your own with only one ingredient needed. There is little need to buy them and they are wayyyyy better made at home.

 **Prep**
5 Mins

 **Cook Time**
30 Mins

 **Serves**
12 Crisps

 **Difficulty**
Easy

Ingredients

1 cup (83 g) cheese, shredded - I prefer Cheddar

Optional seasoning:
  Feel to add a sprinkle of Taco Seasoning, Ranch Seasoning, Italian Seasoning, or Everything but the Bagel Seasoning.

Cooking is an expression of self!

Special Supplies

- Parchment Paper

Gluten Precautions

- If you are buying pre-shredded cheese just make sure you check the ingredients label.

- Spices are used a lot in all types of cooking, but many are processed in facilities where gluten exists. Although they don't 'contain' gluten, please watch for 'may contain' statements on ALL your spices.

- Ensure these are cooked in a non-convection oven as we don't want the air circulating while they bakes.

Directions

STEP 1

Preheat the oven to **300°F (150°C)**. Cover a baking sheet with parchment paper. I prefer to use paper for these to soak up moisture from baking.

STEP 2

Make 12 even mounds of cheese on the parchment paper spaced about 1" (2.5 cm) apart. I like to use my fingers to slightly squeeze the mounds of cheese. If using any seasoning, lightly sprinkle it on top at this time.

STEP 3

Place the tray in the oven for 9 minutes. Remove the tray from the oven. Allow the cheese to cool for 10 minutes. Flip the cheese crisps. Return to the oven. Bake for an additional 8-10 minutes. Watch the crisps carefully at the 7-minute mark as they can turn brown quickly.

STEP 4

Remove the pan from the oven and let the cheese cool on the pan before enjoying. If not serving immediately, store in an airtight container or bag.

Notes

- These are great dipped in sour cream or another gluten-free dip.

- Please watch the cheddar ones carefully, too little cooking and they do not get crispy, but if you bake them too long they will burn. Watch them closely to get them perfect.

- These can be made with Pepper Jack, Mozzarella, or Parmesan cheese. Feel free to blend different cheeses. Please do not use soft or processed cheese slices to make these.

Who doesn't like french fries (aka Hot Chips)? Very few of my friends will turn down fries/chips whether they are baked or fried, homemade or store-bought, seasoned or plain. Some people may say these are a side dish, not a snack, but don't try to tell my kids they are not a snack.

Most people think it is necessary to deep fry them to get a crispy exterior and soft interior, but my method of soaking them first produces the same results without the need for the deep fryer. Season them as desired and enjoy!

FRENCH FRIES
(HOT CHIPS)

 **Prep**
25 Mins

 **Cook Time**
30 Mins

 **Serves**
4

 **Difficulty**
Easy

Ingredients

About 4 large potatoes (1 1/2 lbs or 680 g) - I prefer Yukon Gold, but Russet are also good.

4 tablespoons (60 ml), olive oil divided equally

1 teaspoon kosher salt plus more to taste

1 teaspoon garlic powder

1/2 teaspoon dill weed

1/4 teaspoon onion powder

1/4 teaspoon ground black pepper

Optional Toppings- chives, freshly grated parmesan cheese (or nutritional yeast), seasoning salt, sea salt and black pepper

Be true to yourself.

Special Supplies

- Parchment paper or aluminum/aluminium foil
- Clean cutting board

Gluten Precautions

- Cutting boards are a common source of cross-contact. Please choose a plastic board that is free from any deep grooves and ensure it is scrubbed well with a brush in clean soap and water.
- Ensure these are cooked in a non-convection oven as we don't want the air circulating while these bake.
- Spices are used a lot in all types of cooking, but many are processed in facilities where gluten exists. Although they don't 'contain' gluten, please watch for 'may contain' statements on ALL your spices.

Directions

STEP 1

Preheat oven to **450°F (230°C)**. Drizzle a large parchment or foil-lined baking sheet with 2 tablespoons (30 ml) olive oil, brushing it as needed ensuring it nicely coats the pan.

STEP 2

Wash the potatoes (peel if desired) and slice them into 1/4" (6mm) wide sticks. Place the potatoes in a large bowl, then pour very hot tap water over the top so that it covers the potatoes by at least 1" (2.5 cm). Let sit for 10 minutes.

STEP 3

Drain the potatoes and lay them on a clean towel or paper towel. Dry as completely as possible and return to a dry bowl. Drizzle with the remaining 2 tablespoons (30 ml) olive oil and sprinkle with spices. Toss to coat, making sure the spices and oil are well distributed. Spread the potatoes into a single layer on the prepared baking sheet.

STEP 4

Place in the oven for 15 to 20 minutes, until they start to turn golden underneath. Remove the baking sheet from the oven and carefully loosen the fries/chips and flip them trying to rotate the potatoes around as you flip them. Try to ensure the potatoes return to a single layer and put the pan back in the oven. Continue baking until the fries/chips are as golden and crisp as you like, about 5 to 10 additional minutes. While the fries/chips are hot, sprinkle with any additional and optional toppings and maybe a bit more salt to taste. Enjoy!

Notes

- If using condiments like ketchup and mustard, commonly found in a squeeze bottle, please watch for gluten crumbs that may have been sucked into the tip if it was wiped on bread for example. Please buy or open a new bottle if there is any chance of crumbs.
- Colanders and strainers are notoriously hard to clean and should be avoided. If you decide to drain your potatoes after soaking, I suggest you check out my Tips chapter on page 38 for suggestions on doing this safely. If you tightly squeeze the dishtowel with the potatoes you can get most of the moisture out.
- Place leftovers in an airtight storage container in the refrigerator for up to 3 days and reheat at 400°F for 5-10 minutes watching carefully to prevent burning.

SCHOOL SAFE SNACKS

Many schools limit nuts from entering schools due to allergies. Although many of the snack recipes from the previous chapter are also nut free, this chapter is dedicated to providing a range of tasty and healthy snack options that are suitable for taking to school to serve to kids. All of the recipes in this chapter are still easy to make, require minimal prep time, and are free of gluten, making them perfect to throw together for a school event.

Some of my other recipes in other chapters are also nut free and great for kids. Please see my Fruit Marshmallow Dip in the Appetizer chapter (page 91).

Hard to believe that a cereal made from rice may not be safe for celiacs or gluten avoiders, but your typical Rice Krispies cereal contains Barley Malt which makes it unusable. However, there are certified gluten-free crispy rice cereals that can be found in the Organic or Gluten Free Sections of the store. They may be boxed or bagged, just make sure they are certified gluten-free in the USA. In Canada and more recently in the USA, there are Brown Rice Krispies that are gluten-free and safe to use.

These treats should also be peanut free which makes them good for schools.

 **Prep**
45 Mins

 **Cook Time**
None

 **Serves**
24

 **Difficulty**
Medium

Ingredients

6 cups (300 g) of mini marshmallows

4 tablespoons (60 ml) butter

5 cups (1250 ml or 125 g) crispy rice cereal

1 cup (250 ml or 118 g) dried apple *see my instructions in Gluten Precautions below

1 teaspoon vanilla

11 oz (310 g) caramels

1 tablespoon (15 ml) cream/milk

Dare to be different.

Special Supplies

- parchment paper
- 12 small sticks for handle, around 2-4" (5-10cm) - ie popsicle stick, lollipop stick, straws, unused wooden skewers
- Regular 'Rice Krispies' contain gluten and cannot be used unless you can find Brown Rice Krispies (Canada and new in the USA) which state gluten-free on the box or maybe Rice Puffs in Australia or Rice Pops in the UK. If you visit the health, organic or gluten-free section of your local grocery store, you can usually find a few different brands of gluten-free crispy rice cereal. Gluten-free crispy rice cereal can also be found at natural and health food stores.

Gluten Precautions

- Marshmallows are generally gluten-free. These do NOT have to be certified gluten-free to be safe. They just cannot contain any gluten containing ingredients. Please read ingredient list.

- Ensure your saucepan is free from any deep groves or scratches and please wash it with a clean cloth, dish soap and fresh water prior to use to reduce chance of cross-contact.

- Dried apples can usually be found at your local grocery stores, but can easily be dried at home. Just wash and slice a couple of apples into 1/8" (3mm) thick slices and place them on a parchment-lined baking tray.

  You don't have to peel or core the apple either. I like to slice them horizontally to get a visually appealing star shape in middle. (Place the apple with the core facing sideways and slice from top down - see pictures on right) You can also dip in 1 Tbsp (15 ml) lemon juice mixed in 1 cup (250 ml) water to prevent browning if preferred. Bake at 225°F (105°C) for 45-60 minutes flipping halfway through, until they are dried and edges start to curl up.

- The majority of caramel products are gluten-free. They are not a high-risk item therefore do not require certified or gluten-free labeling. Once again though, please check ingredients list and allergens statement for any wording that mentions containing gluten, wheat, barley, or rye.

- Butter/Margarine is a common source of cross-contact issues. Please be careful to ensure there are no crumb particles.

Directions

STEP 1

If your dried apple pieces are large, break them into smaller pieces - about the size of a pea. Measure out 1 cup. No worries if you are slightly over or under a cup.

Also measure out the crispy rice cereal and set aside.

STEP 2

You can either **A)** melt marshmallows in a microwave - Using a clean glass or microwave-safe bowl add marshmallows and butter. Place in microwave on high for 30 seconds. Stir well and place back in the microwave for another 30 seconds. Stir again. Then continue to heat for 15 seconds at a time until they are fully melted. Stir in vanilla until smooth. OR **B)** I highly recommend melting on the stove. I have had inconsistent results in the microwave.- In a large, clean saucepan over low heat, mix marshmallows and butter. Stir often until melted and smooth. Remove from heat and stir in vanilla. **Please be careful as marshmallows will be extra sticky when hot.**

STEP 3

Stir in the apple pieces and crispy rice cereal and mix well. Even if you have tough hands, you need to let it cool enough for it to hold together when you squeeze it. If it is super sticky and you are unable to handle it, let it cool a little more.   It should be slightly warm. Shape about 1/3 cup (80ml) into a ball or apple shape.   It is highly sticky in the beginning. I find letting it cool a little extra is better. Don't leave it too long though as it will harden too much to shape. You can cover or spray your hands with oil first. Place your chosen type of handle/stick into the center of the ball and then place it on a piece of parchment paper to cool to room temperature.

STEP 4

While cereal balls are cooling, remove caramel wrappers if required, and melt as per package instructions OR I prefer the stove method as you can keep the pan on low to keep the caramel warm while dipping. Place them into a medium saucepan and add 2 tablespoons of milk, cook the caramels over medium-low heat for about 10-15 minutes. Stir constantly until the caramel is fully melted.

STEP 5

One by one, using the attached stick/handle, dip the ball/apple into the caramel and turn the ball as dipping. Be careful the caramel is hot, but ensure it is covered well. I like to use a spoon or small spatula to help turn the ball and lift extra caramel sauce on the ball. I find the stick is never fully secure so this helps maintain the stick position. Then as you lift it, with help of a spatula/spoon, let excess caramel drip off back into pot. Hold it for a few seconds while slowly turning it to let it set a bit before placing it on parchment paper. Then place the ball back onto the parchment paper with the stick standing straight up. As the caramel in the pot gets low you can tip the pot ensuing it runs to one side and then you may have to spread it onto apples using a spoon or knife. Feel free to use any extra caramel to drizzle among all the 'apples' sitting on parchment paper and let cool.

Notes

- Feel free to slightly alter the size of balls/apples.

- If you feel creative and would like to add any other fun items like sprinkles or decorations, please read the packaging to ensure they are gluten-free.

- Ensure you store finished items in an airtight container away from contaminates until ready to serve.

Here is another unique, but sinfully simple snack perfect to take to school. The most difficult part is containing your creativity.

Obviously, you will need to use gluten-free pretzel sticks, but these are usually very common to find and I've yet to have a really bad gluten-free pretzel.

 **Prep**
30 Mins
(allow 30 minutes to set)

 **Cook Time**
None

 **Serves**
20-30

Difficulty
Easy

Ingredients

1 package of gluten-free pretzels

1 cup (240 ml) preferably white baking chips or finely chopped white chocolate (you can sub for regular chocolate, but the white makes them look nicer)

4-5 small packages (0.33 oz or 9.5 g each) Pop Rocks (Fizz Wiz) or popping candy

Life is what you make it.

Special Supplies

- parchment paper
- double boiler or a glass bowl sitting over a pot of simmering water, but not touching the water. You want heat but not direct contact.
- Pop Rocks are common around Halloween, but outside of this time, they can usually be found in candy/sweets stores, convenience stores, and even dollar-type stores.
- Gluten-free pretzels can be found in most grocery stores. Sometimes they are located near regular pretzels, sometimes they can be found in the Organic or Gluten Free section.

Gluten Precautions

- White chocolate and pop rocks are normally gluten-free, but as always, please ensure you read the label to verify.
- Ensure your bowl or pot used on top of a double boiler is free from any deep groves or scratches and please wash it with a clean cloth, dish soap, and freshwater before use to reduce the chance of cross-contact.

Directions

STEP 1

Heat the white melting chips or white chocolate in a double boiler set over medium heat. Keep over heat until fully melted, about 5 minutes. You can melt this in a microwave, but I find the mix cools too quickly making it hard to dip the pretzels.

STEP 2

Once melted, you can either pour the dipping sauce into a tall glass or just leave it in the pot used to melt it and it keeps warm.

STEP 3

One at a time, dip a pretzel into the white melting chips mix or chocolate about halfway down. Allow the excess white mix to drip off. Immediately sprinkle the popping candy onto the pretzel while it is still wet. Set onto a baking sheet lined with parchment paper.

Continue with remaining pretzels. Tilt the glass or melting bowl when necessary to allow the tops of pretzels to fully immerse in white mix.

STEP 4

Allow pretzels to set in fridge for 30 minutes before serving.

Notes

- If you feel creative and would like to add any other fun items like sprinkles or decorations, please read the packaging to ensure they are gluten-free.
- If you can't find pretzel sticks, you can use any shape of gluten-free pretzels.

This unique mix of popcorn, pretzels, Chex cereal, and potato chips/crisps, all coated in caramel is the perfect blend of salt and sweet. Without any nuts, it's the perfect snack for school!

I should warn you that it is extremely addicting and you can easily find yourself with an empty bowl. It is surprisingly easy to make.

CARAMEL PARTY MIX

 **Prep**
15 Mins

 **Cook Time**
5 Mins

 **Serves**
12 cups

 **Difficulty**
Easy

Ingredients

6 cups (750 g) popped popcorn
2 cups (500 ml) Chex type cereal
1 1/2 cups (375 ml) gluten-free pretzels
1 1/2 cups (375 ml) broken ruffled potato chips/crisps

Caramel Sauce
1/2 cup (125 ml or 112 g) unsalted butter
1 cup (250 ml or 213 g) packed brown sugar
1/3 cup (80 ml or 110 g) corn syrup
1/4 teaspoon salt
1 teaspoon vanilla
1/4 teaspoon baking soda/bicarb soda

Aim for the stars.

Special Supplies

- parchment paper
- There are lots of ingredients in this recipe that have gluten and gluten-free options. Please be careful and check the ingredient label on everything you choose and all customizable additives.
- Gluten-free pretzels can be found in most grocery stores. Sometimes they are located near regular pretzels, sometimes they can be found in the Organic or Gluten Free section.

Gluten Precautions

- Baking Soda/Bicarb Soda does not contain gluten ingredients, but can occasionally be found with 'May contain' gluten warnings. Please ensure you check carefully.
- Although they are generally gluten-free, please ensure you check the labels of popcorn and potato chips/crisps to ensure they are safe.
- Ensure this is cooked in a non-convection oven as we don't want the air circulating while this bakes.
- Although corn can be a concern for cross-contact gluten, pure corn syrup is made from highly processed corn and therefore is safe without a 'May contain' statement.
- Many people use a piece of bread in their brown sugar container to keep it soft. Please ensure nothing is or was previously stored in this container to soften it.

Directions

STEP 1

Preheat the oven to **350°F (177°C)** and place a piece of parchment paper on a large baking sheet.

STEP 2

Place the popcorn, cereal, pretzels, and broken-up ruffled potato chips/crisps in a large, heatproof bowl. Measure out all the other ingredients and get them ready for making the caramel as you don't want to leave the caramel sauce unattended.

STEP 3

In a medium saucepan, melt the butter. Add brown sugar and corn syrup. Bring this to a boil as you stir frequently. Reduce to a simmer and let cook for 2 minutes **without stirring**. (Set a timer) Remove saucepan from heat, stir in salt and vanilla. It will bubble up as you are adding liquid to hot sugar. To prevent splatter burns, stir carefully. Add baking soda/bicarb soda and stir vigorously until it gets lighter and creamy in color.

STEP 4

Pour the caramel mixture over the party mix. Stir well. Spread on the prepared baking sheet. Bake in the oven for 2 minutes, then remove from the oven and stir. (It is common for mixing to send pieces over the edge so don't mix in the oven). Then return to oven for another 2 minutes. Remove from oven and let cool. It will set up and become crunchy. Break it up and place it in the serving dish.

Notes

- Every oven is different, please watch the mix while in the oven to ensure the caramel sauce doesn't burn.
- Ensure you stir the mix halfway through baking. I find using a silicone oven mitt and a spatula allows you to mix while not burning your hand.
- Do not substitute the ruffled potato chips for regular ones. Regular chips/crisps are too thin and will likely burn as the mix bakes.

COOKIES/BISCUITS & TREATS

Cookie/Biscuits are an awesome treat for people of all ages. There are many reasons why people enjoy these treats. They are a convenient snack any time of day, they are a great way to satisfy a sweet tooth, and can be a comforting treat during times of stress. They can be a fun and easy food to bake and share with others, making them a great choice for social gatherings and celebrations. Best of all there is no reason why cookie/biscuits and treats can't be part of a gluten-free lifestyle.

If you are not a baker, but need to bring cookie/biscuits to a social event, please review the chapter on 'Last Minute Ideas' (page 155) and 'Reading labels' (page 16) and visit your local organic/gluten-free section at your local grocer.

In this chapter, you'll find a variety of delicious gluten-free cookie/biscuit and treat recipes that are perfect for anyone avoiding gluten. As with other chapters, there is a separate section for all important gluten precautions for each recipe. Whether you're looking for a quick treat to satisfy a craving or want to whip up something special for a party, you'll find some delicious options to choose from in this chapter.

Another treat you can easily find is chocolate/candy bars or candy/sweets. There are many gluten-free versions, but also many contain gluten or have a 'may contain' statement. Please carefully read the ingredients label to determine if it is safe or not.

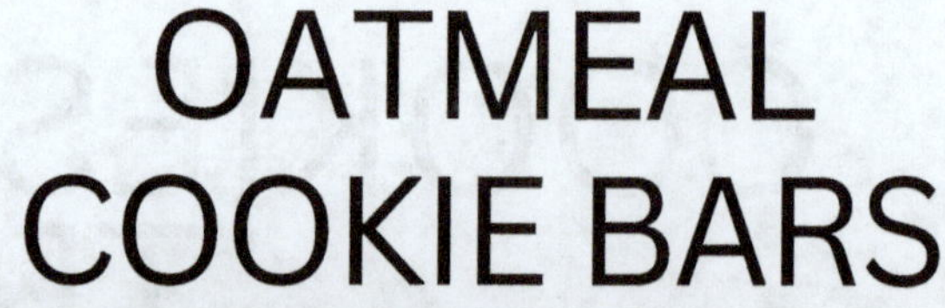

These cookie/biscuit bars are naturally gluten-free treats as they contain no flour that needs to be replaced. The key here though is to use certified gluten-free oats as oats are a high contamination risk. It is very easy to mix these up with your choice of fillings. Our favorite is using dried cherries from our garden.

These treats are by far my most commonly requested treat and recipe by our non gluten-free friends.

 **Prep**
10 Mins

 **Cook Time**
20 Mins

 **Serves**
24

 **Difficulty**
Medium

Ingredients

1 1/2 cups (375 g) peanut butter

1/2 cup (1 stick or 112 g) butter, softened

1 cup (220 g) brown sugar

1 cup (200 g) granulated sugar

3 large eggs, room temperature

1 tablespoon (15 ml) vanilla

1 teaspoon salt

1 teaspoon baking soda/bicarb soda

3 cups (750 ml - 240 g) gluten-free Regular oats * (see note in Special Supplies)

2 cups (500 ml - 160 g) gluten-free Quick oats *   (see note in Special Supplies)

1 cup (250 ml) of choice of Additives - ie dried fruit, M&Ms, chocolate chips, gluten-free Oreo pieces, raisins, caramel pieces, etc.

Believe in yourself.

Special Supplies

- parchment paper
- a large baking sheet with an edge - 12"x 16" (30cm x 40cm) is best. If your baking sheet is smaller, these may rise up and drip over while baking. Suggest you place 80% of batter in 11" x 13" (28cm x 33cm) sheet pan and then place leftovers in a square 8" (20cm) pan, again with parchment paper. See Appendix for tips (pg 166-167) It may require less cooking time. Carefully watch after 15 minutes.

- * NOTE - Certified gluten-free oats are more expensive than regular oats so rather than buying 2 different kinds of oats for this recipe, just put 2 heaping cups of Regular oats in a clean blender and then buzz for a couple of seconds only. You do not want to make flour, but rather just chop the large oat flakes into smaller pieces. You can do this with a knife as well, but make sure your cutting board is cleaned and not wooden as wood can hold gluten.

Gluten Precautions

- Please do not use regular, uncertified oats unless only making for someone avoiding gluten by choice. Chances of cross-contact are high with oats not marked gluten-free. You can find gluten-free oats sometimes in the same sections as regular oats, but more commonly in the gluten-free, organic or health section of the store.

- This is a very thick dough. The easiest way to make these is to use a stand mixer. However, there is a risk of contamination since there are turning parts of the mixer you just can't access to clean. A hand mixer has the same concerns. The safest solution is to mix by hand using a sturdy spoon or spatula. If you choose to use a mixer, please carefully try to ensure there are no residues, especially in areas not easily visible, and disclose that a mixer was used to the recipient.

- Peanut Butter in its natural state is gluten-free but again, please verify the ingredients label and more importantly, ensure there are no crumbs. If in doubt, scrape the top portion off into a separate bowl with a clean spoon, and use the peanut butter underneath. Just ensure to go deeper than a knife could with gluten on it from previous user.

- Baking soda/bicarb soda is only one ingredient and therefore gluten-free. Occasionally there is a 'may contain' statement due to cross-contact.

- If you are using a spray to grease your pan please ensure it is gluten-free as well. Most regular sprays do not have gluten, but there are a few that are meant for baking and include flour to prevent sticking. Avoid using these.

- Using parchment paper on your baking sheet will prevent contact with whatever may have been previously made on this same baking sheet. It also makes it easier and safer to remove these from a baking sheet and cut into serving pieces.

- My favorite way to cut these is with a pizza wheel, but my personal wheel is safe from hidden gluten. You can be more safe cutting these with a long sharp knife. Safe from gluten that is, but please be cautious with a knife.

- Many people use a piece of bread in their brown sugar container to keep it soft. Please ensure nothing is or was previously stored in this container to soften it.

- Ensure this is cooked in a non-convection oven as we don't want the air circulating while this bakes.

- Butter/Margarine is a common source of cross-contact issues. Please be careful to ensure there are no crumb particles.

Directions

STEP 1

Preheat your oven to **375°F (190° C).** Line a 12"x 16" (30cm x 40cm) baking sheet with parchment paper. See Appendix for tips (pages 166 -167)

Add softened butter, peanut butter, and both sugars to a large bowl or stand mixer. Mix vigorously for a few minutes until creamy.

STEP 2

Add eggs, one at a time and mix well. Then add vanilla and mix well.

STEP 3

In a separate bowl, mix regular oats and quick oats together. Add salt and baking soda/bicarb soda and mix again.

STEP 4

Add the oat mix to the peanut butter mixture. It will get hard to mix, but assuming you mixed oats in Step 4, you shouldn't have to mix it long. Just stir until evenly distributed.

STEP 5

Add your choice of an additive - dried fruit, M&Ms, chocolate chips, etc. and mix well.

STEP 6

Carefully scoop the batter onto the baking sheet. I like to place a mound of batter in each corner and then randomly around the rest of the baking sheet. Using a spatula and just wet hands, try to press the mixture around, evenly distributing until flat.

STEP 7

Bake in a preheated oven for 20 minutes. Watch the last few minutes carefully. If it's starting to get brown, remove it from the oven. It will be puffed and quite soft. Do not think it is undercooked. It will flatten and harden as it cools. Just leave it on the baking sheet on the counter for 15-20 minutes.

STEP 8

Once cool, remove parchment from the baking sheet by just sliding it on to your counter. Using a large sharp knife or pizza wheel*, slice as desired. I usually make 2 slices along the long end to make 3 even rows. Then go the opposite way to make 8-10 even slices.

Notes

- * If using a Pizza wheel to slice, please wash it well prior and take special care to ensure the rotating mechanism is clean.   A scrub brush at this location is best.

- Please use your creativity to think of new additives. Just ensure they are gluten-free.

- Ensure you store finished items in an airtight container away from contaminates until ready to serve.

These cookie/biscuits are delightfully soft, sweet, and chewy. They are naturally gluten-free treats as they contain no flour that needs to be replaced.

I could tell you that coconut boosts energy and endurance therefore it can help repair sore muscles after a heavy exercise, but no one is going to believe this little cookie/biscuit is anything more than delicious!

They can be dipped in chocolate for an added treat, but are simple to make and naturally delicious just as is.

COCONUT MACAROONS

 **Prep**
15 Mins

 **Cook Time**
20 Mins

 **Serves**
24

 **Difficulty**
Easy

Ingredients

14 oz (400 g) of sweetened flaked or shredded coconut

7/8 cup (207 ml) of sweetened condensed milk which is equivalent to 3/4 cup plus 2 tablespoons

2 large egg whites

1 teaspoon vanilla

1/4 teaspoon salt

A recipe is a story waiting to be told!

Special Supplies

- parchment paper

Gluten Precautions

- This is a very sticky batter. The easiest way to form these is to use a well-cleaned ice cream scoop.

- If you are using a spray to grease your pan, please ensure it is gluten-free as well. Most regular sprays do not have gluten, but there are a few that are meant for baking and include flour to prevent sticking.

- Using parchment paper on your baking sheet will prevent cross-contact issues. It also makes it easier and safer to remove the cookie/biscuits from the baking sheet.

- The safest way to whip the egg whites is by hand. Obviously, this is very time-consuming and much easier to do with an electric beater. However, please ensure that the entire mixer itself is clean including the area where the beaters attach to the unit. I suggest using a small brush to get in where it is hard to just wipe and is easy for gluten to hide.

- Ensure these are cooked in a non-convection oven as we don't want the air circulating while these bake.

- Metal cooling racks are notoriously hard to clean and should be avoided. I suggest you check out my Tips chapter on page 38 to handle cooling safely.

Directions

STEP 1

Preheat your oven to **325°F (165°C)**. Line 2 clean baking sheets with parchment paper. In a clean, medium bowl, mix together the coconut, sweetened condensed milk and vanilla extract. Set aside.

STEP 2

In another medium bowl, beat the egg whites and salt until stiff peaks form. Use a large rubber spatula to then fold the egg whites into the coconut mixture in thirds. That is, add about 1/3 of the egg whites and stir gently. Then add half of the remaining egg whites to the bowl and fold gently. Finally, add the remaining amount of egg white to the mixture and gently fold. You want to retain the air from whipping the whites.

STEP 3

Using a smaller-sized ice cream scoop or two spoons, form heaping tablespoons of the mixture into mounds on the prepared baking sheets, spacing about 1 inch (2.5 cm) apart. You should be able to get 12 cookies on each baking sheet using a 4 x 3 pattern.

STEP 4

Bake for 20 minutes, rotating and turning the pans until the tops and edges are golden. I would start checking after 18 minutes to prevent overcooking like mine in the photo.

STEP 5

Let cool on the pans for a few minutes, then transfer to a wire rack to cool completely.

Notes

- Please use your creativity to think of ways to change it up. Maybe dipping in chocolate. Just ensure anything added is gluten-free.

- Ensure you store finished items in an airtight container away from contaminates until ready to serve. Suggest you use parchment paper between layers. These can easily be frozen once cool for about 3 months. Just let them thaw naturally at room temperature.

If you like your cookie/biscuits a bit on the soft side you will love these blossoms. The trick to getting them to stay soft is to make them without flour. No need to find any special gluten-free flour.

These peanut butter blossoms only need a few simple ingredients that you will likely already have on hand in your kitchen.

Best of all, they don't taste gluten-free.

Prep

15 Mins

(plus an hour to chill)

Cook Time

10 Mins

Serves

24

Difficulty

Easy

Ingredients

1 cup (250 g) peanut butter

1/2 cup (100 g) granulated sugar

1/3 cup (70 g) brown sugar

1 large egg, room temperature

1/4 teaspoon salt

1 teaspoon vanilla extract

2 tablespoons (30 ml) granulated sugar for rolling cookie/biscuit balls in

24 Hershey's Chocolate Kisses, unwrapped (or your favorite chocolate pieces)

PEANUT BUTTER BLOSSOMS

Mind over matter.

Special Supplies

- parchment paper
- Plain/Traditional Hersey's Chocolate Kisses or similar gluten-free chocolates

Gluten Precautions

- Peanut Butter in its natural state is gluten-free but again, please verify the ingredients label and more importantly, ensure there are no crumbs. A new jar is best. At minimum, scrape off the top portion into a separate bowl with a clean spoon. Just make sure you go deeper than any knife that may have been used previously.
- Using parchment paper on your baking sheet will prevent contact with whatever may have previously been made on this same baking sheet. It also makes it easier and safer to remove cookie/biscuits.
- Ensure these are baked in a non-convection oven as we don't want the air circulating while these bake.
- Not all Hershey's Kisses are gluten-free. The traditional, silver-wrapped ones are normally safe, but always check the label.
- Metal cooling racks are notoriously hard to clean and should be avoided. I suggest you check out my Tips chapter on page 38 to handle cooling safely.
- Many people use a piece of bread in their brown sugar container to keep it soft. Please ensure nothing is or was previously stored in this container to soften it.

Directions

STEP 1

In a clean medium bowl, mix all the ingredients except for the additional 2 tablespoons of sugar and Kisses chocolate. Chill for at least an hour. Chilling will make them easier to roll into balls and helps maintain shape as they bake.

STEP 2

After the dough is chilled, preheat the oven to **350°F (177°C)**. Line 2 clean baking sheets with parchment paper.

Roll dough into about 1" (2.5 cm) balls. You should be able to get 24 balls.

STEP 3

Place the 2 tablespoons of sugar in a bowl and roll each ball into the sugar and then place on the baking sheet. You should have 12 balls on each baking sheet.

STEP 4

Bake for 8 -10 minutes or until they are starting to brown on the bottom. Use this time to ensure all chocolate kisses are unwrapped.

STEP 5

Remove cookie/biscuits from the oven and immediately place a chocolate kiss, or your favorite chocolate, on top and press down slightly. The heat from the cookie/biscuit will warm the chocolate and soften it.

Let cool on the pans for a few minutes, then transfer to a wire rack to cool completely.

Notes

- Ensure all your ingredients are at room temperature when mixing. Although the mixture does need to chill, mixing anything in cold changes the overall texture when baking and they will likely come out flat.
- Ensure you store finished items in an airtight container away from contaminates until ready to serve. Suggest you use parchment paper between layers.
- These can easily be frozen once cool for about 3 months. Just let them thaw naturally at room temperature.

This recipe only has a few ingredients but the results are amazing. They are rich and deliciously chewy. It will require you to buy or make almond flour, but everything else is likely already in your kitchen. If almond flour is unavailable in your area, I have provided instructions for making your own and have also made these using gluten-free certified oat flour.

These wonderful little bites are dairy free but are not suitable for anyone with a Nut allergy.

PEANUT BUTTER BROWNIES

 **Prep**
15 Mins

 **Cook Time**
30 Mins

 **Serves**
9-12

 **Difficulty**
Easy

Ingredients

1 cup (250 g) peanut butter (Not natural - there should be no oil sitting on top)

3 large eggs at room temperature

3/4 cup (150 g) brown sugar

1 cup (120 g) almond flour (you can buy, make your own or you can use oat flour - see Special Supplies section for notes)

Every meal is a journey!

Special Supplies

- parchment paper
- an 8"x 8" (20cm x 20cm) pan. You can use 9"x 9" (23cm x 23cm) pan as well, but the brownies will be thinner requiring careful attention to cooking time as you will likely need less time. You can use glass or a metal pan but ensure it is cleaned well prior to use.
- You can make your own almond or oat flour. Just place about 120 grams (a heaping cup) of blanched almonds or oats, in your blender and buzz for about 3-5 minutes until a fine, powdery flour is achieved. Don't go too far as you'll end up with butter instead. Ensure blender is clean.
- Please also do not use natural peanut butter where there may not be salt or sugar added and the oil is separated and rests on top. These will not be the same.

Gluten Precautions

- Almond flour is naturally gluten-free, but avoid it if the bag states 'may contain' wheat.
- These taste much better using almond flour, but if you cannot find almond flour and decide to make your own flour with blanched almonds or oats, please ensure they state gluten-free and there is no 'May contain wheat' statement on the bag.
- If you do make your own almond flour or oat flour, please ensure the blender is very clean including running it before use with water and a few drops of dish soap to clean the areas beneath the blades that could hide residual gluten.
- Peanut Butter in its natural state is gluten-free but again, please verify the ingredients label and more importantly, ensure there are no crumbs. A new jar is best. At minimum, scrape off the top portion into a separate bowl with a clean spoon. Just make sure you go deeper than any knife that may have been used previously.
- This is a very thick and sticky dough. The easiest way to make these is to use a stand mixer. However, there is a risk of contamination since there are turning parts of the mixer you just can't access to clean. A hand mixer has the same concerns. The safest solution is to mix by hand using a sturdy spoon or spatula. If you choose to use a mixer, please carefully try to ensure there are no residues, especially in areas not easily visible, and disclose that a mixer was used to the recipient.
- Even though you will need to ensure your pan is clean, please still use the parchment paper. Please see the Appendix for Tips (pages 166-167).
- If you are using a spray to grease your pan please ensure it is gluten-free as well. Most regular sprays do not have gluten, but there are a few ones that are meant for baking and include flour to prevent sticking. Avoid using these.
- Ensure this is cooked in a non-convection oven as we don't want the air circulating while this bakes.
- Many people use a piece of bread in their brown sugar container to keep it soft. Please ensure nothing is or was previously stored in this container to soften it.

Directions

STEP 1

Preheat your oven to **325°F (165° C).**

Line a clean 8" x 8" (20cm x 20cm) pan with parchment paper. See Appendix on pages 166-167 for tips.

STEP 2

In a large bowl, mix peanut butter and sugar with a large, sturdy spoon or spatula. Mix well. If necessary, the peanut butter can be warmed slightly in a microwave to make it easier to mix (suggest about 30 seconds on a medium setting). Add beaten eggs and mix well again. Add almond (or oat) flour to the bowl and mix again. Blend as best you can.

The dough will be thick and sticky but is manageable with a sturdy spatula or spoon. It is easier to mix with a hand or stand mixer, but I seldom use one as there is less to clean up with just a bowl and spatula. This is my mixture to the right.

STEP 3

Once the batter is mixed well, transfer it to the prepared pan. Use a spatula (if the batter is too sticky you can oil or moisten the spatula) try to spread evenly around the pan and smooth the top.   If you have an offset spatula this is made even easier.

STEP 4

Bake for 30 minutes. The brownie should be puffed, but still firm to the touch. Make sure you do not overbake as it will end up drying out. If you are using a large pan, start watching at about 20 minutes for doneness.

STEP 5

Remove the pan from the oven and allow it to sit for 30 minutes at room temperature to finish setting up. When it is no longer hot to the touch, use the parchment paper to lift the entire brownie to a cutting board.

Slice as desired. I suggest cutting it into 9 pieces.

Notes

- You can cut these any size you want. If serving adults as a main dessert, cutting in 9 pieces results in a good serving size. If this is for kids, maybe cut it into 12 pieces.

- If you feel creative and would like to add any other fun items like sprinkles or maybe add chocolate chips or nuts to the batter, please read the packaging to ensure they are gluten-free.

- Ensure you store finished items in an airtight container away from contaminates until ready to serve.

GLUTEN
FREE

APPETIZERS
Entrees

Appetizers/Entrees are usually finger foods that are served before a meal. They may range from very simple to very complex, depending on the occasion and the time you devote to making them. They don't have to take a long time though.

Some options that you can easily just pick up are things you may already be serving and not realize they are gluten-free. For example, a **Shrimp Ring**. This traditional appetizer is found at most grocery stores. Shrimp is naturally gluten-free. However, you do have to watch the cocktail sauce. I would say 80% of sauces are gluten-free, but a quick look at the label will confirm. You should be able to find one that is safe and even if not, you can find a separate cocktail sauce in your condiment section of the store that can be used instead of the gluten-containing one.

Another quick and easy option includes **tortilla chips**. A verified gluten-free tortilla chip can be paired with almost any dip. A great choice for an appetizer is a **Hummus dip**. Again, traditional hummus is gluten-free but you will need to confirm with the label.

In addition to tortilla chips, let's not forget **tortilla scoops/cups**. You can find these beside the tortilla chips in your local store. These provide a great vessel for filling with your favorite flavors - egg and cheese, spinach and cream cheese, taco cups, vegetables, etc. Just confirm filling ingredients are gluten-free.

Our family was offered these appetizers at a get-together once and we went out and bought a portable smoker the following week just to make these ourselves. They were simple and delicious. Originally, we only ever made these on our smoker. Then one day it was too cold to venture outside, therefore I decided to take a stab at making them in the regular oven. They were just as delicious!

Despite the simplicity of this dish, it is unique and wonderfully flavored. It is hard to just eat one.

 **Prep**
10 Mins

 **Cook Time**
20 Mins

 **Serves**
10-12

 **Difficulty**
Easy

BACON WRAPPED PICKLES

Ingredients

24 pickle spears (6 large pickles sliced vertically to get 4 long thin quarters)

6 -12 slices bacon, regular thickness
Do not use thick cut (see Notes)

1 tablespoon (15 ml) of Montreal steak seasoning (or your favorite steak spice)

1/2 cup (125 ml) ranch dressing (optional)

Discover the magic of cooking!

Special Supplies

- Parchment paper or foil
- Toothpicks

Gluten Precautions

- Please ensure all utensils and pans are clean.

- Don't be surprised to learn that some bacon has gluten. You can usually find ones though that are gluten-free. Just read the labels.

- Spices may be processed in facilities where gluten exists. Although they don't 'contain' gluten, please watch for 'may contain' statements on ALL your spices.

- Ensure these are cooked in a non-convection oven as we don't want the air circulating while these bake.

- Salad dressings can be subject to thickeners and vinegars that are dangerous for gluten. If you are deciding to use a ranch dressing for dipping, please read the labels.

Directions

STEP 1

If you haven't already done so, slice your pickles into quarters vertically so you have 4 long pieces.

STEP 2

Preheat the oven to **400°F (200°C).**

Start by cutting a single piece of bacon in thirds.
Wrap a 1/3 piece of bacon around the pickle spear using a spiral motion. You want the bacon to wrap down the length of the pickle, but you don't want too much overlap as it won't cook evenly. Please see my picture below.

Note: Usually 1/3 pieces work well, but if pickles are larger or bacon is a little leaner, you may need to cut the rest of the bacon in half to get it wrapped around the pickle. Although it hasn't happened for me yet, if the bacon is less costly, the 1/3 piece may stretch more and be too long. Therefore, if any of the wrapped bacon is more than 2 layers thick, cut the remaining bacon pieces into quarters for smaller pieces.

Once you know what works for your bacon and pickles, cut the rest of the bacon and wrap the remaining pickles with the bacon securing them with a toothpick. Place each pickle spear on a baking sheet lined with parchment paper or foil.

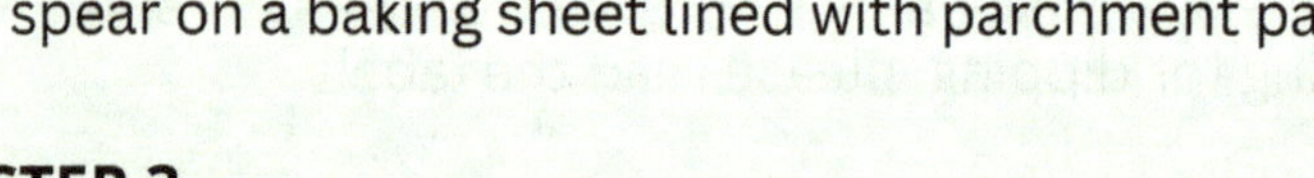

STEP 3

Place the baking sheet in the preheated oven. After about 5 minutes, remove the pan and sprinkle with your favorite steak spice. If you don't wait to sprinkle the seasoning until the fat starts to warm, it will not stick to the bacon. Return to the oven and bake for another 15 minutes or until the bacon is crispy.

We like to just eat them plain, but you can serve them with Ranch Dressing or any gluten-free dipping sauce would likely be great.

Notes

- <u>Don't use thick cut bacon.</u> You want the bacon crisp and thick cut will take much too long to crisp up in the oven.
- If you're looking for smaller bites, cut your pickle quarters in half to make them shorter. You may need to increase your amount of bacon though.
- If you don't like spice, you don't have to use it.
- High heat and bacon grease can be dangerous. Please watch carefully.

Stuffed mushrooms are a delicious and easy appetizer that are sure to impress your guests. They are simple to make and you can serve these tasty treats hot from the oven and watch as they disappear in no time!

These mushrooms are loaded with a creamy artichoke parmesan mixture. They are so indulgent, no one at the party will be able to resist this vegetarian, low-carb, gluten-free appetizer!

INDULGENT STUFFED MUSHROOMS

 **Prep**
25 Mins

 **Cook Time**
20 Mins

 **Serves**
16

 **Difficulty**
Medium

Ingredients

16 oz (450 g) white button, cremini or baby bella mushrooms

1 tablespoon (15 ml) olive oil

1/3 cup (80 ml) diced onion

1/4 teaspoon salt

1/4 teaspoon pepper

6 oz (185g) cream cheese, softened and cubed

1 1/4 cup (125 g) freshly grated parmesan cheese, divided

2 tablespoons (30 ml) sour cream

3/4 teaspoon garlic salt

12 ounce (340 ml) marinated artichoke hearts, drained and chopped

Cooking is an Adventure!

Special Supplies

- Aluminum/Aluminium Foil or parchment paper

Gluten Precautions

- Please ensure your pots and all utensils are clean. Cover your baking tray with aluminum/aluminium foil.
- Ensure they are cooked in a non-convection oven as we don't want the air circulating while these bake.
- If using a cooking spray, ensure it is gluten-free. Yes, some sprays are specifically made for baking and contain flour to prevent sticking.
- Although less commonly subject to cross-contact with gluten, ensure there are no crumbs in your sour cream container.

Directions

STEP 1

Preheat the oven to **400°F (200°C)**. Line a baking sheet with foil.

Prepare the mushroom caps by gently washing them. Pat dry on a dish towel. Remove the stems by using a small paring knife or a spoon to go around the stem. Then gently twist the cut stem and pop it out. Chop the mushroom stems and transfer the mushroom caps to the foil-lined baking sheet.

STEP 2

Add olive oil to a large, deep sauté pan over medium heat. Add the chopped stems, onions, salt, and pepper to the pan and cook for 5-6 minutes, or until the onion is soft and translucent.

Reduce the heat to low and add the artichokes, cream cheese, 1 cup parmesan, sour cream, and garlic salt.   Stir to combine until the cream cheese has melted.

STEP 3

Transfer the stuffing to the prepared mushroom caps, filling as much as possible. Please see Notes section for handling extra filling. Sprinkle the tops with the remaining parmesan cheese.

Bake for 16-18 minutes, until the mushrooms are tender and the filling is golden, hot, and bubbly. Serve immediately. Makes about 16-20 large or 24-28 small mushrooms.

Notes

- For an added crispy topping, sprinkle some crushed plain, gluten-free potato chips/crisps on top of the mushroom caps before the extra parmesan.
- You can make the filling a few days in advance and store in fridge. When ready to bake, fill as per Step 3.
- I have never made these without having extra filling. I like to place it in some extra foil and then place it in the oven with the mushrooms. When hot, serve in a bow as a dip for tortilla chips or something else.
- Dice everything really fine as it makes it easier to fill the mushroom.

Despite the ease of creation, this recipe will provide a wonderful healthy snack for both adults and kids. You can mix up the fruit to find whatever is seasonal. It requires no baking and is ready in 10 minutes.

Once again, it is not only gluten-free but also peanut free which makes it good for schools.

 **Prep**
10 Mins

 **Cook Time**
NONE

 **Serves**
many

 **Difficulty**
Super Easy

Ingredients

8 oz (250 g) cream cheese - softened

3/4 cup (175 ml) cherry yogurt or flavor of choice

8 oz (1 L) frozen whipped topping (about 3-4 cups), thawed*

7 oz (200 g) marshmallow creme or fluff**

Fresh Fruit

* Whipped topping is NOT the same as whipping cream. If you cannot find frozen whipped topping, please see the Special Supplies section on the next page for homemade whipped topping instructions.

** If marshmallow creme/fluff is not available, you can replace with vanilla frosting but use less as it is much sweeter. I would suggest using 1/2 the amount and adjust to taste and desired thickness.

MARSHMALLOW FRUIT DIP

Special Supplies

- If you can't find frozen whipped topping you can make some at home. I have 2 methods **A)** Whip 2 cups (500 ml) of very cold whipping cream with 2 Tbsp (30 ml) instant GF vanilla pudding. When slightly thickened add 1/4 cup (60 ml or 28g) powdered sugar and 1 tsp vanilla extract. Continue whipping until thick with medium peaks. Use in the recipe as is or refrigerate. OR **B)** Sprinkle 1 tsp of gelatin over 1/4 cup (60 ml) cold water, stir, and then let sit for 3 minutes. Next microwave it for 5 seconds, stir and microwave another 5 seconds or until the mixture has liquified. Let it cool. Combine 1 1/2 cups (375 ml) of very cold whipping cream with 1 Tbsp (15 ml) powdered sugar and 1/2 tsp vanilla extract. Mix slowly at first and then increase to medium and mix until visibly thicker. While continuing to beat with the mixer, slowly add the gelatin mixture. Once all gelatin is incorporated, increase the mixer to high and whip until medium peaks form. Use in the recipe or refrigerate.

Gluten Precautions

- Marshmallow Fluff/Creme is generally gluten-free, but please read the jar for ingredients. These do NOT have to be certified gluten-free to be safe. They just cannot contain any gluten-containing ingredients.

- The safest way to whip ingredients is to do this by hand. This is more time-consuming and is much easier to do with an electric beater. However, please ensure that the entire mixer itself is clean including the area where the beaters attach to the unit. I suggest using a small brush to get in where it is hard to just wipe and is easy for gluten to hide.

- Yogurt is generally gluten-free, but some flavors are thickened with flour so please read the ingredients. These do NOT have to be certified gluten-free to be safe. They just cannot contain any gluten-containing ingredients.

Directions

STEP 1

In a large bowl, beat cream cheese and yogurt until blended.

STEP 2

Fold in whipped topping and marshmallow creme.

Serve with fruit.

Notes

- Ensure you store in the fridge away from contaminates until ready to serve.

GRAPE JELLY MEATBALLS

These delicious meatballs are the perfect party appetizer! Simply mix 4 ingredients and throw them in a Crock Pot and let it do the rest. Serve the meatballs hot from the crock pot with toothpicks for an easy and crowd-pleasing snack. These work wonderfully with either beef or chicken meatballs.

They can also sit for hours warm in the crock pot as guests arrive or are served all at one time. They are also suitable as a Potluck dish. They are very flexible.

 **Prep**
5 Mins

 **Cook Time**
3 hours

 **Serves**
10-12

 **Difficulty**
Easy

Ingredients

32 oz (1 kg) frozen fully cooked meatballs - beef or chicken

1 cup (250 ml) grape jelly/jam

1 1/2 cups (375 ml) barbecue sauce

2 tablespoons (30 ml) chili garlic sauce

You are capable of great things

Special Supplies

- A large, clean slow cooker or crock pot.

Gluten Precautions

- Please ensure your crockpot and all utensils are clean.
- Don't be surprised to learn that some frozen meatballs contain bread crumbs as a binder agent. Read the labels. You can usually find ones that are gluten-free or you can make your own. See the notes section for tips on making your own.
- Also carefully watch your BBQ sauces. You can find both gluten-free ones and ones with gluten in the same section of your store. Read your labels to verify. This is the same for chili garlic sauce.
- I have never seen any jam or jelly that has gluten, however, it is commonly subject to cross-contact from someone spreading toast or bread. Please consider using a fresh jar or at minimum, scrape off the top layer going deep enough to capture a knife length of crumbs with a clean spoon and remove. Also always verify the label ingredients.

Directions

STEP 1

Mix the jelly, BBQ sauce, and chili sauce together. Add meatballs to slow cooker and pour this mixture over top.

STEP 2

Cook on low for 3-4 hours, stirring halfway through cooking. Once the meatballs are cooked, turn the slow cooker to warm and keep warm until ready to serve.

Garnish with parsley or chives if desired.

Notes

- Feel free to make your own meatballs. Just don't use any gluten ingredients. I suggest that you make sure they are fully cooked first or they tend to fall apart in the sauce.

- If you don't like spice, you can use less or even leave out the chili garlic sauce. It's not that spicy though and is delicious mixed with jelly.

MAIN DISHES

If you have been learning from my basic ideas and principles, you'll find limitless tasty options for gluten-free main dish cooking.

- Choose plain meat, chicken, turkey, fish, ham, vegetables, legumes, and eggs as they are all naturally gluten-free.
- Watch out for bottled and boxed foods as many shelf-stable foods have additives that contain gluten. If you're buying store-bought packages just read the label to make sure it's gluten-free.
- Luckily, starches like rice and potatoes are naturally gluten-free as well, but if you're swapping out for gluten-free pasta, choose wisely. As mentioned in some recipes, not all gluten-free pasta has a great texture so I try to choose ones that have a mix of gluten-free flours rather than just one main flour.
- Make your dressings and sauces: Like other shelf-stable foods, some store-bought salad dressings and sauces contain gluten. While you can buy gluten-free versions, it's usually cheaper (and tastier) to make your own!

I'll admit I am not a Vegetarian BUT, I have often found delicious recipes that don't contain meat. My Buddha Bowl recipe in this chapter can easily be adapted to be vegetarian. Although I don't specifically have an entire chapter dedicated to Vegetarian recipes, based on the information I have provided on how to read labels and prepare your work area to be gluten-free, you should be able to search the internet for a recipe that you like and then make it safe for your guest.

Here are a few delicious and satisfying recipes that could become family favorites despite them being gluten-free. I have tried to ensure this section has something different to offer. Whether you're looking for a quick and easy weeknight dinner or a special meal to impress guests, you'll find a recipe in this section that is sure to be a winner. Get ready to explore a few tasty main dish options and discover new favorites!

You've likely been eating chicken fingers for many years. They are loved by many different age groups and especially picky eaters tend to like these when nothing else will do.

Best of all, you can easily make these gluten-free. You can just use one of the suggested gluten-free coatings in your regular recipe and follow the gluten precautions. The added taste and texture from the suggested toppings make these delicious and easy to make. I suggest pairing it with the French Fries recipe in the Snack chapter (page 63).

 **Prep**
30 Mins

 **Cook Time**
20 Mins

 **Serves**
4-6

 **Difficulty**
Medium

Ingredients

1 lb (450 g) boneless, skinless chicken breast

1 large egg, beaten

2 tablespoons (15 ml) mayonnaise

1 teaspoon garlic powder

1 teaspoon onion powder

Kosher or Sea salt to taste

Pepper to taste

1 1/2 cups (375 ml) coating of choice (see below)

1/2 cup (125 ml or 45 g) grated parmesan cheese - optional

Coating choices - You can buy gluten-free bread crumbs or make any of the following using a plastic bag and a rolling pin - gluten-free cracker crumbs **OR** gluten-free pretzels **OR** Tortilla chips **OR** Doritos **OR** gluten-free certified cereals (like crispy rice cereals or other less sweet ones) **OR** Potatoes Chips/Crisps (even flavored ones are perfect as long as they are gluten-free). You can combine a few of these as well.

Don't be afraid to fail.

Special Supplies

- A large, clean baking pan
- Aluminum/Aluminium foil or parchment paper
- A clean cutting board
- You can use a variety of coatings as noted in the ingredients section, but please verify anything you want to crush is gluten-free. If in the USA and using a cereal, please remember to only use certified gluten-free ones, not just one with the words gluten-free.

Gluten Precautions

- Cover your baking pan with aluminum/aluminium foil.
- If using a cooking spray, ensure it is gluten-free. Yes, some sprays are specifically made for baking and contain flour to prevent sticking.
- A clean cutting board is important to slice chicken. Preferably not a wooden one as it has more areas to hide gluten. In a pinch, you can place a piece of parchment paper over the cutting board, but just be careful not to cut through the paper.
- Ensure this is cooked in a non-convection oven as we don't want the air circulating while these bake.
- Spices are used a lot in all types of cooking, but many are processed in facilities where gluten exists. Although they don't 'contain' gluten, please watch for 'may contain' statements on ALL your spices.
- Mayonnaise is normally gluten-free and it can be found in both a jar and a squeeze bottle. However, it is commonly used for bread so a new jar or bottle is preferred as a gluteny knife can be dipped a long way into the jar so you can't simply remove the top portion. As well, if the tip of a squeeze bottle has been wiped on bread, gluten crumbs can then be sucked back into bottle when sides are released, contaminating it with gluten. If you are 100% sure the tip is safe, then you can use it.

Directions

STEP 1

Preheat the oven to **375° F (190°).**   Cover your baking sheet with foil or paper. Set aside.

STEP 2

Slice chicken breast into strips. Try to get them all the same size to ensure they cook evenly. You should be able to get 3-5 strips per breast.

STEP 3

Beat eggs, mayonnaise, and seasonings in a separate bowl.

Place the coating mix in another bowl. If using parmesan, add it to this bowl.

STEP 4

Dip each chicken strip in the beaten egg, covering both sides. Let the egg mix drip briefly and then dip in the crumb coating. Press lightly on the crumbs to ensure they adhere to the chicken. Place strips on the covered baking pan. Spray lightly with cooking spray.

STEP 5

Bake in the oven for 10 minutes. Flip each strip over and bake an additional 5-10 minutes. Internal temperature of chicken should be 165°F (74°C).

STEP 6

Serve with a ketchup bottle or your favorite gluten-free dip. Enjoy!

Notes

- The easier way to create the crumb coating would be to place your choice of coating ingredient in a blender. I choose to recommend just crushing them manually due to the fact there is not a great deal of them to crush and they don't need a fine texture. However, using your blender is a potential source of gluten. If you decide to use your blender, please pre-wash it extra carefully including running the blender with water and dish soap and then allowing it to dry completely.

- I love how much extra flavor potato chips/crisps add. My favorite choice is an all dressed flavor, but whatever your favorite chip is would be awesome to add to a chicken strip. Most are gluten-free, but please check the ingredients label to ensure.

- You can use boneless, skinless thighs for these strips as well, but I would suggest cutting them in half and making more round, less long, and thin strips. They should cook in the same amount of time.

- An excellent side dish to serve with these is simple french fries/chips. Again, most are gluten-free, but some seasoned ones will have gluten requiring careful inspection of the ingredients label. Please see my Snack chapter for a gluten-free french fry recipe (page 63).

- I haven't provided a dipping sauce as there are many choices, but a simple mix of half ketchup and half mayonnaise or Ranch dressing is a good choice to go with these strips. Please see pages 38- 39 for tips on safely using condiments.

  - These are also easy to pan-fry. Just add a couple of tablespoons of oil to a pan and heat for a few minutes. Fry each chicken piece for about 3-4 min per side. Do not over-crowd pan. You may have to fry it in a few batches.

Maybe you automatically think that spaghetti and sauce are not an option as it contains gluten, right? Well, traditional pasta DOES contain gluten, but not only does gluten-free pasta exist, but it is amazingly good.

Spaghetti made from gluten-free grains is a delicious alternative for those who are intolerant or sensitive to gluten. It can be paired with many of the same sauces and toppings as regular spaghetti, such as meatballs, vegetables or just sautéed in olive oil and garlic. After you've found the right gluten-free pasta, you can serve your gluten-free spaghetti with a sprinkle of grated Parmesan cheese for a satisfying and flavorful meal.

SPAGHETTI

 **Prep**
5 Mins

 **Cook Time**
20 Mins

 **Serves**
6

 **Difficulty**
Easy

Ingredients

1 box (about 1 lb or 340 g) of gluten-free spaghetti noodles

1 jar (about 24 ozs or 640 ml) of your favorite pasta or tomato sauce

Grated parmesan cheese

Salt and Pepper

Live with purpose.

Special Supplies

- A large, clean pot, possibly a colander (see Precautions) and spaghetti spoon.
- Gluten-free spaghetti noodles are pretty common in your local grocery stores. They can usually be found alongside regular pasta or found in the Organic/Gluten Free section of the store. I would suggest a brand that combines more than one flour type (such as Rice and Corn or Rice, Corn, and Quinoa) is best. There are really good all rice or all corn ones, but there are also less good ones. It is usually safer to get a mixed flour one for the best results.

Gluten Precautions

- Strainers and colanders are notoriously hard to clean of gluten. I suggest you avoid any fine mesh strainers. A regular, larger hole strainer is better but could still be a problem. To drain your pasta safely, please check out my Tips chapter on page 38, for suggestions on doing this safely.
- Obviously, the spaghetti noodles need to be gluten-free, but also check your pasta sauce and spices. Most pasta sauces are gluten-free, but as always, please read the ingredients label carefully.
- Taste-wise, gluten-free spaghetti is amazingly similar to regular pasta. There is a big difference however, in cooking it. Gluten-free spaghetti goes from a perfect 'al dente' to 'fall apart/overdone' in a surprisingly small amount of time. The taste will still be amazing however, it will not look the same with noodles that will fall apart. I would suggest that you cook the pasta according to package directions or slightly less than what you would normally cook it.
- If using canned pasta sauce, please wash your can opener prior to use.

Directions

STEP 1

Start to cook the spaghetti according to the package directions. As mentioned, err on the side of undercooked as gluten-free pasta gets overcooked really quickly. Suggest setting a timer to ensure you don't go over the suggested time.

STEP 2

As the pasta is cooking, add the pasta sauce to a small pot and place it on the stove on low to warm as the pasta cooks.

STEP 3

Once the pasta is cooked to al dente, strain the water and place in a serving bowl.

STEP 4

Serve the sauce over the warm spaghetti, sprinkled with freshly grated parmesan cheese. Feel free to consider serving pasta and sauce separately as my kids sometimes like a lot of sauce and sometimes they prefer none.

Notes

- Feel free to mix up the pasta as well. Gluten-free pasta can be found in almost all the same forms as regular pasta. You can mix it up and try penne, fusilli, or plain macaroni.
- If you do happen to be making regular pasta at the same time, ensure they are cooked in different pots, water and with separate utensils and colanders.
- You can definitely add in some gluten-free meatballs or fry some ground/minced meat in a frypan and add pasta sauce directly to this pan with the meat.
    - I would recommend you don't add olive oil to the noodles during or after cooking – this makes the noodles get a starchy/slimy film on the outside. Instead, you can toss the pasta with some of this sauce after cooking if necessary.

Tacos are a popular Mexican dish that can be made quickly, healthy and satisfying for dinner. The best part is they can be easily customized for individual tastes. If your child or a guest doesn't like tomatoes, they don't have to put them on their taco. You can go in another direction as well and just buy tortilla chips for the base and then cover them with all the toppings for a salad.

There is an abundance of gluten-free Mexican items available at most grocery stores — just pay special attention to the pre-mixed taco seasonings, sauces, tortillas, and beans for hidden gluten.

 **Prep**
20 Mins

 **Cook Time**
15 Mins

 **Serves**
4-6

 **Difficulty**
Easy

Ingredients

1 packet (1 oz or 28 g) taco seasoning (gluten-free) or mix spices as described in Gluten Precautions on page 132.

A package of either soft corn tortillas or gluten-free flour tortilla AND/OR hard taco shells

1 tablespoon (15 ml) vegetable oil

1 lb (454 g) ground/minced beef OR fish OR chicken, cut into small strips or pieces.

Toppings - suggestions

Grated cheese - your favorite

Shredded Lettuce   Shredded Cabbage

Diced Onions   Diced Tomatoes

Sliced Sweet Peppers   Diced Cucumbers

Sour Cream   Salsa

Avocado

Nothing brings people together like good food.

Special Supplies

- Gluten-free flour OR corn tortillas are pretty common. They can usually be found near the regular tortillas or in the Organic/Gluten Free section of the store. For hard taco shells, they can usually be found in the Mexican aisle of your local grocery store. Please verify that they are gluten-free. I like using a combination of a hard shell wrapped in a soft tortilla.
- Aluminum/Aluminium foil to warm flour tortillas.

Gluten Precautions

- Please ensure your skillet, cutting board and all utensils are clean.
- Gluten-free flour tortillas are something that have been an ongoing disappointment to me. I have found lots that I think are delicious, but only if you warm them first. When gluten-free tortillas are not warm, they do not wrap nicely and will usually end up ripping. I would suggest if using gluten-free flour tortillas or even corn tortillas that you **warm them before serving**.
- Almost all corn tortillas are naturally gluten-free. The same goes for almost all hard taco shells, but there are always exceptions, therefore it's important to read labels.
- Most packaged taco seasoning is gluten-free, but reading ingredients is still necessary. If you cannot find a gluten-free version, use the recipe in the Gluten Precautions section on page 132.
- Spices are used a lot in all types of cooking, but many are processed in facilities where gluten exists. Although they don't 'contain' gluten, please watch for 'may contain' statements on ALL your spices.
- A clean cutting board is important. Preferably not a wooden one as it has more areas to hide gluten. In a pinch, you can place a piece of parchment paper over the cutting board but just be careful not to cut through the paper when dicing toppings.

Directions

STEP 1
Slice, dice and grate all selected toppings. Place in separate bowls on the table.
Preheat your oven to **200°F (95°C)**.

STEP 2
Heat oil in frying pan over medium heat. Add your choice of protein and fry until fully cooked. This should take 5-7 minutes regardless of your choice.

STEP 3
While your meat is cooking, wrap the gluten-free flour or corn tortillas in foil and place in the oven for 5-10 minutes (TIP - add a slightly wet paper towel to the pack). For hard tacos, follow the instructions on the package ensuring the baking sheet is covered with foil or parchment paper. If making my preferred hard and soft tacos, you will be baking hard shells at a higher temperature. Therefore, put the hard tacos in the oven first and double wrap the soft tortillas in foil, and then place them in the oven for the last few minutes.

STEP 4
Following the instructions on the taco seasoning package, add seasoning to the pan with your choice of meat and the suggested amount of water. If you made your own seasonings, add to the pan with 2 tbsps (30 ml) cornstarch (* In the UK and Australia, please use cornflour) and 1/4 cup (60 ml) water. Stir until thickened - about 5 minutes.

STEP 5
Put cooked meat into a bowl and place on table along with warmed tortillas. Let everyone prepare their own tacos! Enjoy!

Notes

- I love to place a flour tortilla flat on my plate, Then place a hard shell taco on top of it. Fill the hard shell as desired. If you've loaded too many topping in your hard shell, you can place it just slightly out on the flour tortilla. Then fold up the flour tortilla around the hard shell. As your hard taco shell cracks as you bite it, the toppings stay contained nicely in a soft tortilla.
- The smaller you dice the toppings, the easier it is to fill the taco.

Buddha Bowls, also known as grain or power bowls, are a very trendy type of dish that is made by combining a variety of colorful and nutritious ingredients in a single bowl. They typically include protein, grains, and vegetables with a sauce to tie them all together. Best of all, you can customize them any way you want. Want a **vegetarian meal**? Omit the meat. Avoiding peanuts, choose a different sauce. Hate peas? Don't include them.

These are individual bowls and therefore very customizable. Go wild!

BUDDHA BOWL

 **Prep**
20 Mins

 **Cook Time**
30 Mins

 **Serves**
4-6

 **Difficulty**
Medium

Ingredients

1 lb (454 g) **chicken** - breasts or boneless thighs OR your favorite **fish** cut into small, bite-sized pieces.

Sauce #1 - suggested for Chicken

1/3 cup (80 ml) lime juice

1/4 cup (60 g) smooth peanut butter

3 tablespoons (45 ml) tamari or gluten-free soy sauce

1 tablespoon (15 ml) sesame oil

2 teaspoons (10 ml) honey

1 teaspoon hot sauce

1 clove garlic, minced

1 tablespoon (15 ml) minced ginger

Sauce #2 - suggested for Fish

3/4 cup (about 175 ml or 183 g) sour cream or Greek yogurt

2 teaspoons (10 ml) lemon or lime juice

1 garlic clove, peeled
PLUS either
2-3 tablespoons (30-45 ml) fresh dill or (2-3 tsp dried)
-OR-
1/4 teaspoon chili powder or to taste
2 hot peppers – Fresno or Jalapeno, seeded and roughly chopped

Salt and pepper to taste

Bowl Options

1 1/2 cups (375 ml) cooked rice or quinoa ; 2 large sweet potatoes diced and baked ; 1 cucumber diced ; 2-3 cups (500-750 ml) spinach, chopped ; 1 1/2 cup (375 ml) frozen corn, thawed ; 1 1/2 cup (375 ml) frozen peas, thawed ; 1/2 cup (125 ml) diced onions

Other Toppings

Grated cheese - your favorite, chopped cashews or peanuts
Diced Tomatoes, Peppers, Avocado, Lettuce, Kale, Squash of any kind.

Special Supplies

- A large, clean skillet and clean cutting board.
- Gluten-free soy sauce or tamari. This may be harder to find in the regular section of the grocery store, but should be easily found in the Organic/Gluten Free Section.
- Aluminum/Aluminium foil (if baking anything in the oven)

Gluten Precautions

- Please ensure your skillet and all utensils are clean.
- Quinoa is subject to cross-contact and should be marked gluten-free.
- Soy sauce normally has gluten, as wheat is usually one of the first ingredients. Sometimes you can find gluten-free soy sauce in your Chinese/Asian section of a grocery store. You'll have to read labels extremely carefully. You can usually find a gluten-free version in the Organic/GF Section. Tamari is often used for soy sauce and as well as ones labeled soy seasonings.
- If using a blender, please ensure it is cleaned extremely well.
- A clean cutting board is important. Preferably not a wooden one as it has more areas to hide gluten. In a pinch, you can place a piece of parchment paper over the cutting board, but just be careful not to cut through the paper when dicing toppings.
- Peanut butter and honey in their natural state are gluten-free but again, please verify the ingredients label and more importantly, ensure there are no crumbs. A new jar is best.

Directions

STEP 1

If you are using toppings that require cooking - follow the package instructions for rice and quinoa. Items like sweet potato or squash should be diced small and roasted in oven at **400°F (200°C)**. Both will need about 20 minutes to cook. Continue with other steps while these cook.

STEP 2

Slice, dice and grate all other toppings you have chosen to include. Place in separate bowls on the table. Don't forget a topping like chopped nuts. They add a unique crunch to the bowl.

STEP 3

Make the sauce. For Sauce #1, it may be easier to mix if peanut butter is warmed in the microwave first, then add the remaining ingredients and mix well. Set aside.   For Sauce #2, I recommend putting all the ingredients in a blender and mix for 30 seconds to provide a smooth sauce. If you don't have a blender, just mince the garlic and peppers and mix well.

STEP 4

Heat the oil in a large, clean skillet. Add the Chicken or Fish and fry until cooked through - about 7 min/side for chicken, about 2 min/side for Fish. Turn the heat off.

STEP 5

Put protein choice into a bowl and place on the table along with any cooked toppings. Drizzle the sauce over the bowl. Let everyone prepare their own bowls!

Notes

- These really are customizable. I would suggest you have a starch, a protein and vegetables to make a complete meal.
- The chicken and peanut butter combination is my favorite, but there are many different sauces you can use. Just search the internet and check all ingredients for gluten.
- The smaller you dice the toppings, the easier it is to fill the bowl.

Lentil casserole is a delicious and healthy vegetarian option that is perfect for a hearty and satisfying meal. I first made it when my meat-avoiding niece came for dinner and we all found it to be a flavor explosion. My meat-loving husband, even finished off the leftovers the next day.

Whether you're looking for a quick and easy weeknight dinner or a dish to feed a crowd, lentil casserole is sure to be a hit. My daughter, who doesn't like casseroles OR melted cheese, actually ate a full serving as I intentionally left off half the cheese as seen in my picture.

LENTIL CASSEROLE

 **Prep**
10 Mins

 **Cook Time**
30 Mins

 **Serves**
6

 **Difficulty**
Easy

Ingredients

2 tablespoons (30ml) olive oil

1 rib celery - finely diced

1 medium onion - finely diced

1 (28 oz or 796 ml) can diced tomatoes

1 (19 oz or 540 ml) can lentils, drained

1 (19 oz or 540 ml) can kidney beans, drained

1 clove garlic, crushed

2 tablespoons (30 ml) chopped fresh rosemary

salt and pepper to taste

1 1/2 cups (375 ml) shredded cheddar cheese - (or your favorite vegan melting cheese)

Inspire your palate with your cooking!

Special Supplies

- An oven safe fry pan OR a clean fry pan and casserole dish. The oven is only used to melt the cheese on the top of the dish so it's not essential in any case.

Gluten Precautions

- Ensure all your bowls and utensils are clean.
- Dried lentils themselves are gluten-free however, they are subject to cross-contact concerns and should be labeled gluten-free. Canned lentils do not have to be labeled gluten-free as they are checked during processing but if given an option, please choose ones marked gluten-free.
- Please don't use a cast iron pan for this dish. Although it is oven safe and holds heat wonderfully, it can also hold gluten and you shouldn't wash cast iron with soap and water or you'll destroy any seasoning you've built up. I would suggest using an oven-safe metal fry pan right from the beginning. If you don't have an oven-safe pan, then fry it up in a regular pan and then switch to an oven-safe clean casserole dish before placing it in the oven. Again, broiling the cheese is nice, but optional.
- Colanders and strainers are notoriously hard to clean and should be avoided. To drain your beans and/or lentils, I suggest you check out my Tips chapter on page 38, for suggestions on doing this safely.
- Please carefully clean your can opener prior to use.
- Please also carefully clean your grater before use. There are lots of hiding spots for gluten.

Directions

STEP 1

Heat a large, oven-safe frypan over medium heat. Add the olive oil.
When the oil is hot, add the diced celery and onions to the pan and sauté for 2-3 minutes.

STEP 2

Add the drained beans, drained lentils, and diced tomatoes to the pan along with the rosemary and garlic. Season with salt and pepper.

STEP 3

Bring the pan to a boil, then once it is boiling reduce the temperature to low to gently simmer for 20 minutes. The mixture will thicken up a lot.

STEP 4

Set your oven to broil.

STEP 5

Cover the oven-safe pan with shredded cheese (Or pour the lentil and bean mixture into a small casserole dish and cover it with the shredded cheese)
Broil the dish for 2-4 minutes or until the cheese melts and begins to crisp.

Notes

- If your vegetarian guest doesn't eat cheese, just substitute with vegan-friendly, melting cheese or leave it off entirely and skip Steps 4 and 5.

SIDE DISHES

As the name implies, side dishes are to be served alongside your main dish. There are many good side dishes out there and you could easily make an entire meal just from side dishes. Making them gluten-free isn't that hard especially if you stick to the basics, like **naturally gluten-free potatoes, rice, and vegetables.** Also, consider **grains** such as Amaranth; Cornmeal; Grits; Polenta; Flax; Millet; Quinoa; Sorghum; Teff as well as Beans and Lentils that are all marked gluten-free due to cross-contact concerns. Also, **seeds and nuts** in their natural, unprocessed forms without a 'may contain' statement.

Watch out for bottled/boxed foods as many shelf-stable foods have additives that contain gluten. If you're buying store-bought packages of seasoned rice mixes, couscous, canned beans, etc., just read the label to make sure it's gluten-free. Make your dressings and sauces: Like other shelf-stable foods, some store-bought salad dressings and sauces contain gluten. While you can buy gluten-free versions, it's usually cheaper (and tastier) to make your own!

The problem once again is trying to make a naturally gluten-free dish in an environment that may not be gluten-free.
I think I have provided the information in previous chapters to allow you to make some choices of your own, but I have included the following recipes for you to follow as well. A mashed potatoes recipe may not be needed, but since it is a big part of my Full Dinner meal suggestions, I have included them to make things easier on how to avoid cross-contact.

I have included gravy as a side dish as it is a big part of many dinners, especially holiday or fancier dinners. It is surprisingly simple to make gluten-free and many people already make gravy gluten-free and don't realize it. As always, there is more than just using gluten-free ingredients therefore, I offer other steps to ensure it is safe for all.

There are also gluten-free gravy mixes you can buy so I have included instructions for these too. I often make gravy from scratch but still utilize the gravy mixes.

 **Prep**
10 Mins

 **Cook Time**
10 Mins

 **Serves**
6-8

 **Difficulty**
Easy

Ingredients

3-4 cups (1 L) liquid - broth, water, stock, drippings

1/4 cup (60 ml) cornstarch*

1/4 cup (60 ml) cold water

Salt and Pepper (to taste)

Optional
- few tablespoons of cream, milk or butter
- a teaspoon of dried herbs of choice - sage, thyme, etc.
- 1 teaspoon each of onion and garlic powder

AND/OR

1-2 packages of prepackaged gluten-free marked gravy mixes

* In the UK and Australia, please use Cornflour

# GRAVY

When you cook a roast, no matter if it's turkey, chicken, beef, or lamb, you should end up with plenty of browned drippings and fat when it's finished cooking. The "drippings" are browned juices and fat which provide a lot of flavor to any gravy you make from these drippings.

Make today count.

Special Supplies

- A clean gravy dish (well technically you can use any serving dish for gravy including right out of the pot you make it in, but a gravy boat is nice)
- If desired, gluten-free gravy mixes can be found in most grocery stores along side regular gravy mixes. They normally have some sort of gluten-free stamp on them but you can just check ingredients label too.

Gluten Precautions

- Please clean your cooking and serving dish and utensils well.

- Obviously if you are using a premade gravy mix, it should be clearly marked gluten-free or nothing concerning listed on the ingredients label.

- Do not make gravy with drippings from a gluten stuffed or seasoned meat.   Gluten is NOT killed with heat and will transfer to gravy.

- Spices are used a lot in all types of cooking, but many are processed in facilities where gluten exists. Although they don't 'contain' gluten, please watch for 'may contain' statements on ALL your spices.

- If using broth or some sort of stock, please ensure it is clearly marked gluten free or ingredients label shows nothing concerning for gluten.

Notes

- Fat from the drippings will add lots of flavors, but too much fat will only just float on top of the gravy making it unattractive to serve and use. If your drippings have lots of fat floating on top, use a spoon to try and remove this to a bowl before you use the drippings for gravy.

- Using the water from boiling potatoes or vegetables adds an extra flavor (and I like to think nutrition 😉) to your gravy.

Directions

STEP 1

If you are just making gravy from a gluten-free packaged mix, just follow the instructions on the package and ensure everything else is clean. One package usually makes 1 cup gravy.

STEP 2

You can make gravy in your roasting pan directly if it was clean and suitable initially (i.e. you did not have to use foil). If you used foil, then just pour the roasting liquids into a separate pot. Add any additional liquids necessary until you have the amount of liquid needed. I like to use liquids from boiling potatoes or vegetables as it adds extra flavor. In any case, add liquids and then heat until boiling on the stove top.

STEP 3

As the liquids get hot, season as you like. I would err on the side of caution as you can always add more seasoning after it is thickened and you can taste it. I like to add a couple of premade gravy mixes to the liquid at this stage and mix it in. They do mix better with cooler liquid. Pre-made packages usually only make a cup of gravy each thus not enough to thicken your gravy, but it does provide a good flavor base.

STEP 4

Mix cornstarch with cold water to dissolve completely. I state about 1/4 c of each, but if you think you have more liquid than 3 cups, then increase the cornstarch. You just really need to add enough water to make cornstarch liquidy ensuring it doesn't make lumps in your gravy. Please note that you should not mix your cornstarch and water too early as they have a property to them that will thicken on their own the longer it sits.

STEP 5

When the liquid is boiling, slowly pour about half of the cornstarch slurry into the liquid and stir until it returns to a boil. Although it takes a minute to reach its full thickness you should be able to determine how much more cornstarch slurry to add. Keep doing this until you are satisfied with the thickness. Remember it needs to boil a short time before it reaches its full thickness. If you make a mistake and add too much, simply add more water to thin it out.   Taste and adjust seasoning as desired.

STEP 6

Your gravy is now ready to be consumed. It may not be perfectly smooth but a sieve is not safe to use. You can try to use a new piece of cheese cloth or maybe a coffee filter but these may not work well. Just use a slotted smooth to remove any large lumps.

Potatoes are naturally gluten-free. Great!
Most people know how to make mashed
potatoes. It's a very common side dish
however, it is also a dish commonly subject
to cross-contact.

It is one of those dishes that those gluten-
intolerant guests shake their heads at as it is
easy to keep gluten-free, but most will skip
enjoying it as they just don't know.
Therefore, I thought it was important to
highlight how to make it safe. Even if you
choose to follow your own recipe, please just
follow my suggestions on how to keep it safe
and make your gluten-free guest happy.

MASHED POTATOES

 **Prep**
5 Mins

 **Cook Time**
20 Mins

 **Serves**
4

 **Difficulty**
Easy

Ingredients

1 1/2 lbs (680 g) potatoes

1/2 teaspoon salt

4 tablespoons (60 ml) milk

3 tablespoons (43 g) butter or margarine

Salt and Pepper

Choose to be happy.

Special Supplies

- a clean potato masher.

Gluten Precautions

- This recipe is super easy to ensure it's gluten-free. There is no mixer to worry about and only one pot, one dish, and some sort of masher to ensure are **clean**. The biggest concern with gluten will be to **ensure your butter or margarine container is free from contaminates**. I can't stress this enough. Most households have at least a few crumbs in their container.

- If you decide to just make instant mashed potatoes, please just check the box carefully. Although potato flakes are usually gluten-free, some boxed instant ones have gluten added in flavorings. Please read the label and take the same precautions with butter contamination.

Directions

STEP 1

Cut potatoes into smaller pieces. The smaller you cut them, the quicker they cook. Key is to make them all about the same size so they cook evenly. Place into a medium size sauce pan and cover with cold water by at least an inch.

Peeling the potato is a personal choice. I prefer to leave mine with the peel on as there are lot of nutrients under the skin and fiber, but obviously they look a lot nicer without the skin. Don't tell my kids though that people make them unpeeled.

STEP 2

Place on the stove on high and when they come to a boil add salt, reduce heat to maintain a boil and boil for about 20 minutes or until they can be pierced easily with fork.

While potatoes are boiling, place milk and butter in a microwave safe bowl and warm in microwave until butter is melted.

STEP 3

Once the potatoes are soft, drain the water and return the potatoes to the same pot. Pour the warmed milk/butter into the pot and mash with a potato masher until creamy. Add salt and pepper to taste.

Notes

- Heating the milk and butter might seem unnecessary, but they will blend more easily into the warm potatoes, making them creamier and softer. It's worth the effort.
- Always start potatoes in cold water. If you start with hot water then the outside of potatoes starts to cook before the centre of the potatoes gets warm creating uneven cooking.

This recipe requires slightly more effort than just plain, roasted potatoes, but the results are much more unique and delicious and it can be well worth the effort. My kids ask for it often.

These potatoes are crispy on the outside and incredibly tender and melty on the inside. You will really enjoy these noteworthy potatoes!

MELTING POTATOES

 **Prep**
15 Mins

 **Cook Time**
60 Mins

 **Serves**
4-6

 **Difficulty**
Medium

Ingredients

About 4 large potatoes - I like Russet

4 tablespoons butter (56 g) - melted

6 tablespoons butter (84 g) - not melted

1 cup (250 ml) gluten-free chicken broth

2 garlic cloves, thinly sliced or chopped

1/2 teaspoon Italian seasonings

Salt and Pepper

Make the best of every moment.

Special Supplies

- a 9"x 13" (23cm x 33cm) metal baking pan with high sides or rim. Please do not use glass. When you add a cool liquid to a hot pan, the glass can crack from the quick temperature change.
- Gluten-free chicken stock is not a specialty item and can usually be found in the soup aisle. It doesn't matter if you choose a version that is canned, boxed or dry, just please check the label to ensure it's gluten-free as many do have gluten.

Gluten Precautions

- Please ensure your baking pan is clean. Using parchment paper doesn't really work in this recipe as it is very liquidy. You can try to form aluminum/aluminium foil around and up the sides of your pan to be extra careful.
- As mentioned above in Special Supplies, chicken broth should be checked for gluten.
- Ensure this is cooked in a non-convection oven or without the convection setting as we don't want the air circulating while this bakes.
- Spices are used a lot in all types of cooking, but many are processed in facilities where gluten exists. Although they don't 'contain' gluten, please watch for 'may contain' statements on ALL your spices.
- Butter/Margarine is a common source of cross-contact issues. Please be careful to ensure there are no crumb particles.

Directions

STEP 1

Preheat Oven to **400°F (200°C)**.

Wash and then slice the potatoes about 1 inch (2 1/2 cm) thick. It is your personal choice on whether you peel the potatoes. Place cut potatoes in a large bowl.

STEP 2

In the bowl with potatoes, add the 4 tablespoons of melted butter and seasonings. Mix and then spread evenly into the 9"x 13" pan. Once again, do NOT bake these in a glass dish as the cooler broth may crack the hot glass in the next step.

STEP 3

Bake for 20 minutes. Then flip the potatoes slices and bake for another 20 minutes. Flip potatoes for a third time and then add enough of the chicken broth to the pan to go about 1/2 way up the potatoes slices. Scatter the garlic through out the pan. Cut the remaining butter into small pieces and distribute on top of potatoes in the pan. Place back into oven for 15 minutes.

STEP 4

Check to ensure potatoes are fork tender and remove pan from oven. Spoon the sauce in the pan over the potatoes before serving

Notes

- Ensure you cut potatoes in even slices to ensure even baking.

This fresh and easy Pasta Salad is gluten-free and packed with crisp vegetables.

This cold pasta salad is beautiful to look at with the mix of fresh vegetables and pasta but is also delicious mixed with the Italian dressing. It is super easy and quick to prepare and a perfect side dish to feed any crowd.

 **Prep**
15 Mins
(plus an hour to marinade)

 **Cook Time**
10 Mins

 **Serves**
6-8

Difficulty
Medium

PASTA SALAD

Ingredients

12 oz (400 g) gluten-free rotini or fusili - even better if you can find tri-colored fusilli

1 large english cucumber, chopped

1 medium each red, orange, and yellow bell pepper, chopped

2 cups (340 g) grape tomatoes, halved

1/2 medium red onion , chopped

1 cup (250 ml) black olives, sliced

1 cup (250 ml) Italian salad dressing

Food nourishes the soul!

Special Supplies

- Gluten-free Rotini (Fusilli) noodles are pretty common in your local grocery stores. They can usually be found alongside the regular pasta or in the store's Organic/Gluten Free section. I would suggest a brand that combines more than one flour type (such as rice and corn or rice, corn, and quinoa) is best. There are really good all rice ones, but there are also less good rice ones. Getting a mixed flour pasta usually provides better results. If you can find a tri-color rotini it makes the salad look nicer, but it doesn't change the taste, therefore if you can only find regular-colored pasta, it is not a problem. There is lots of color provided by the vegetables.

Gluten Precautions

- Please ensure your Italian dressing is gluten-free.
- Taste-wise, gluten-free pasta is amazingly similar to regular pasta. There is a big difference however in cooking it. Gluten-free pasta goes from a perfect 'al dente' to 'fall apart/overdone' in a surprisingly small amount of time. The taste will still be amazing, however, it will not look the same if it breaks apart. A little extra bite to a pasta salad will not be an issue. I would suggest that you cook the pasta according to package directions, less 1 minute as this salad is served cold.
- Please clean and check your pasta strainer or colander well. It is best if you avoid any fine mesh strainers as these are notoriously hard to clean. A regular, larger hole strainer is better but please see page 38 for tips on making it even safer.

Directions

STEP 1

Boil the gluten-free rotini according to package directions, minus about 1 minute to keep the noodles from getting mushy.

STEP 2

While the pasta is boiling, chop the bell peppers, cucumber, tomatoes, onion, and toss them into a large bowl with the sliced black olives.

STEP 3

Drain and rinse the pasta under cold water to stop the cooking process before adding them to the chopped veggies.

STEP 4

Add the Italian dressing. Gently mix everything in the bowl to combine. The pasta salad needs to marinate and chill in the fridge, for a minimum of 30 minutes before serving. It's better if it can sit for a few hours. Serve cool or at room temperature.

Notes

- Ensure you cut all the vegetables evenly to ensure it looks nice when finished.
- Since it has no meat or dairy, it will last longer than other cold pasta salads. You can store it in the fridge for up to a week, making it a perfect side dish.

Vegetables and potatoes are naturally gluten-free and very easy to prepare. Another amazing way to make them delicious, but still safe for those gluten intolerant, is to roast them in the oven. Roasting is a healthier cooking method that helps retain nutrients and can bring out the natural sweetness and flavor. As well, the caramelization that occurs during roasting results in aesthetically pleasing dish that is sure to impress.

These are easy to personalize with your favorite seasonings. Some like the simplicity of just salt and pepper, but feel free to spice it up.

 **Prep**
10 Mins

 **Cook Time**
approx 30 Mins*

 **Serves**
4

 **Difficulty**
Easy

ROASTED VEGETABLES OR POTATOES

Ingredients

4 cups (1 L) total of any chopped vegetable. About 1 cup (250 ml) per person. See below for suggested vegetables and times.

2 tablespoons (30 ml) olive oil

Salt and Pepper

Optional
   1 teaspoon each of Onion Powder, Garlic Powder, Italian Seasoning, Paprika, Thyme, Rosemary, etc

*Asparagus – 20 minutes
  Bell Peppers – 20 minutes
  Broccoli – 25 minutes
  Brussels Sprouts (halved) – 25 minutes
  Butternut Squash – 30 minutes
  Cabbage (cut into 1-inch thick slices) – 30 minutes
  Carrots (cut into 1-inch chunks or baby carrots)- 30 minutes
  Cauliflower – 25 minutes
  Green Beans – 20 minutes
  Kale – 15 minutes (it doesn't need to be in a single layer)
  Onions – 35 minutes
  Potatoes (approx 1" (2.5cm) cubes - 35 minutes

Special Supplies

- Parchment paper or aluminum/aluminium foil

Gluten Precautions

- This recipe is super easy to ensure it's gluten-free. There is no mixer to worry about and only one dish to ensure is clean.   The biggest concern will be your spices. As many are processed in facilities where gluten exists, please watch for 'may contain' statements on ALL your spices.

- Ensure this is cooked in a non-convection oven as we don't want the air circulating while this bakes. If you want to cover or wrap entirely in foil, they will be safer but they will not get as crisp

Directions

STEP 1

Preheat oven to **400° F (200°C)** and place parchment or foil on a rimmed baking sheet.

Wash and prepare your chosen vegetables or potatoes. Some need to cut smaller, some do not. If you are cooking multiple vegetables together you need to determine whether you want to add some quicker cooking vegetables at different times OR you can cut some larger vegetables into smaller pieces than suggested to reduce their cooking time.   The key is to either make everything a size that will ensure they all cook the same amount of time or you plan to cook at different times. For example, if you are cooking carrots or squash which take a little longer together with bell peppers and asparagus, then slice the carrots a little smaller than the suggested 1" (2.5cm) and cook together OR you can place the peppers or asparagus into the oven 10 minutes afterwards so they are all done in 30 minutes after first vegetables went in oven.

STEP 2

Whether you choose to cook them all at same time or different times, add olive oil, seasonings, and your choice of herbs to vegetables and use your hands to mix well. Then spread them evenly out on the foil. Try to stir them about halfway through the cooking process. Don't forget to add the quicker cooking vegetable to oven at a later time if you've chosen this method. For example, mix in some asparagus, 10 minutes after you put carrots in the oven.

Roast until tender. See times in ingredients list.

Notes

- I find the 400F temp is perfect for vegetables but if you are cooking with another item in the oven, you can increase or decrease the temp for vegetables you just need to also adjust cooking time accordingly. i.e. if increasing the temp by 25F, decrease cooking time by 5 min or vice versa.

  - Feel free to add or remove seasoning based on your likes. Also consider serving with sour cream or cheese.

Quinoa is a complete protein, making it a great alternative to rice, while beans are a good source of fiber and protein making the nutritional value of this side dish high.

Flavor can be easily customized and it can be prepared well in advance making it very convenient. In about 30 minutes, you can have an amazing side dish or maybe even a complete meal ready to serve.

QUINOA BEAN SALAD

 **Prep**
20 Mins
(plus 30 min to marinade)

 **Cook Time**
15 Mins

Serves
6-8

 **Difficulty**
Easy

Ingredients

1 cup (250 ml) quinoa (uncooked)

1 can (15 oz or 540 ml) black beans, drained and rinsed

1 1/2 cups (375 ml) English cucumber, quartered and sliced

1 bell pepper, small diced (red, yellow or orange)

1 cup (250 ml) canned corn, drained

1/4 cup (60 ml) sliced green onion (white and light green part only)

FOR THE DRESSING

1/4 cup (60 ml) olive oil

1 teaspoon ground cumin

1 teaspoon fine-grain sea salt (or to taste)

1/4 cup (60 ml) freshly squeezed lime juice (about 2 limes)

1 tablespoon (15 ml) apple cider vinegar

1 tablespoon (15 ml) sugar (optional)

1 clove garlic, minced

1/8 teaspoon ground cayenne pepper (or to taste)

Special Supplies

- Quinoa can be found alongside rice and other grains in your local grocery store.

Gluten Precautions

- Although Quinoa is gluten-free, there is a chance of cross-contact therefore, please ensure it states gluten-free on the package
- Please clean your serving dish and utensils well.
- Not normally a high source for cross-contact, but please carefully wipe the cutting edge on your can opener. If the last thing you opened contained gluten, then this can cross-contact the current cans you need to open.
- Spices are used a lot in all types of cooking but many are processed in facilities where gluten exists. Although they don't 'contain' gluten, please watch for 'may contain' statements on ALL your spices.
- Colanders and strainers are notoriously hard to clean and should be avoided. To drain your beans and/or corn, I suggest you check out my Tips chapter on page 38, for suggestions on doing this safely.

Directions

STEP 1

In a medium sauce pan, cook the quinoa according to package instructions. Place cooked quinoa in a large bowl to cool.

STEP 2

While the quinoa is cooking, drain and rinse the black beans and corn, then prepare the cucumber, bell pepper and green onion.

STEP 3

Whisk together all dressing ingredients in a small bowl.
Add the vegetables and black beans to the large bowl with the quinoa, then pour the dressing on top and stir until well combined.

STEP 4

If you have time: let the salad marinate for about 30 minutes before serving to let the flavors blend.

Notes

- Ensure you cut all the vegetables a reasonable size making it is easier to serve and look nice when finished.
- Store the leftovers in an airtight container in the fridge of up to 4 days.
- Feel free to substitute some of the vegetables. I love adding avocado or grape tomatoes.

This is the dressing/stuffing I grew up on. I've tried quite a few newer recipes, but they had a lot more ingredients and were more work so I always return to this one from my childhood. I call this a dressing as I no longer stuff my turkeys, but the terms are interchangeable these days. Normally stuffing is something that is cooked inside the cavity of an animal and a dressing is cooked separately. As this is separate, I will continue to call it a dressing.

Whatever you want to call it though, it is delicious.

 **Prep**
15 Mins
(plus an hour drying time for bread)

 **Cook Time**
2 hours

 **Serves**
6-8

 **Difficulty**
Easy

STUFFING/ DRESSING

Ingredients

1 loaf (450- 600 g) of gluten-free bread

1 medium onion, chopped

1/2 cup (112 g) butter, (1 stick)

1 teaspoon onion powder

1 teaspoon garlic powder

1 teaspoon ground thyme

1 teaspoon poultry seasoning

1 teaspoon salt (or to taste)

1 teaspoon pepper

Optional - turkey neck

Optional - 1 cup (250 ml) chicken broth

Nothing is impossible.

Special Supplies

- Aluminum/Aluminium foil
- There are many gluten-free bread brands nowadays and I've made this recipe with expensive as well as the cheapest available. As the dressing is best with dry bread, it's not imperative that you know which bread is best. I would suggest you select a mid-range bread - not the cheapest, but also not the most pricey.

Gluten Precautions

- Please clean your mixing bowls, serving dishes, and utensils well.
- Butter/Margarine is a common source of cross-contact issues. Please be careful to ensure there are no crumb particles.
- Spices are used a lot in all types of cooking, but many are processed in facilities where gluten exists. Although they don't 'contain' gluten, please watch for 'may contain' statements on ALL your spices.

Directions

STEP 1

Slice a full loaf of gluten-free bread in 1" (2.5 cm) pieces. They do not have to be equal sizes and l like it better when they are more random-sized. The smaller pieces stick together and get crispier and the larger pieces stay individual. If you have time, if you can dry the bread its even better. Either let it air dry for a couple hours on your counter top or preferably, place in your oven on an aluminum/aluminium baking pan at **250°F (120°C)** for an hour, stirring occasionally.

STEP 2

Melt 1/2 cup butter in a fry pan on medium low heat. Add one medium onion that has been diced. Sauté the onion slowly until softened then add the seasonings. These can be adjusted to your personal taste. If you like sage, add some in. If you don't like thyme, leave it out. Salt and Pepper to taste.

STEP 3

When onion is soft, dump the entire contents of pan onto the bread pieces and mix well. Optional - If you like your dressing moist, drizzle with some or all of the chicken broth. There is nothing raw in this stuffing allowing you to taste it often and adjust accordingly.

STEP 4

Place everything on a large piece of aluminum/aluminium foil. I like to include the turkey neck wrapped with the stuffing for extra flavor, but this is completely optional. Ensure the foil is wrapped tightly around the dressing. If using thinner or a smaller piece of foil, I would suggest double wrapping it. Place in the oven with turkey for the last couple hours of cooking. You will need 2 hours if you've included the neck. Before serving, just dump the entire foil pack into a bowl to serve.

Notes

- If you include the turkey neck in the dressing, ensure it is cooked thoroughly.
- Store the leftovers in an airtight container in the fridge of up to 4 days.

Growing up we only ever had Yorkshire puddings on special occasions. It was a rare treat though and I LOVED them. When my family went gluten-free, I tried for years to replicate my idea of what they should be like and I had lots of failures. There are so many different gluten-free flour blends and it was hard to get consistent results.

Then one day someone suggested I replace the flour with cornstarch and voila, they were perfect in every way. They had a crispy exterior and a beautiful hollow center just waiting for the gravy. Never would I have believed you could create such tasty Yorkshires with only 3 ingredients. My search was over.

YORKSHIRE PUDDING

 **Prep**
5 Mins
(plus 30 minutes rest for batter)

 **Cook Time**
25 Mins

 **Serves**
12

 **Difficulty**
Medium

Ingredients

7 oz (200 ml) milk - I use 2%

4 large eggs

1 cup less a tablespoon (130 g) cornstarch*

Shortening/Fat/Oil for muffin tin (6-12 teaspoons)

*(cornstarch is the highly processed form of corn flour used in North America and is usually known as cornflour in the UK or Australia)

Special Supplies

- a metal 12 cup muffin pan (Metal retains heat for these to rise better)

Gluten Precautions

- Please clean your muffin tin, serving dish and utensils well.
- Verify your cornstarch has no gluten contaminates.
- If using shortening like Crisco, please ensure it is not contaminated from previous use.

Directions

STEP 1

In a large bowl (I like to use a large 4-cup measuring glass), place milk and add eggs. Beat well with a whisk. Add cornstarch and continue to whisk carefully until everything is blended well. Set aside as you want this mix to sit for at least 30 minutes. Continue with the next step while you wait.

STEP 2

Place about 1/2 - 1 teaspoon of shortening or oil in each cup of a 12-cup muffin pan. Place the muffin tin into a **425°F (220°C)** oven to heat up for at least 20 minutes. You want the oil to be extremely hot.

STEP 3

As quickly as you can, BUT as carefully as you can, remove the hot muffin tin from the oven and fill each muffin cup about 2/3 full with the mix from Step 1. You should have enough to fill all 12 cups. If you think you'll run a little short, just fill the last few ones with a little less. Return the muffin tin to the hot oven as quickly as possible. Do not open the door again for at least 20 minutes.

STEP 4

The Yorkshires are done when they have risen high above the muffin tin and are golden brown and crispy to the touch. Remove from oven and serve.

Notes

- Ensure these are cooked well as if they are undercooked, they will deflate slightly after removing from oven.

  - You can skip the mixture resting for 20-30 minute before baking but they will not rise as tall and will be much more dense.

POTLUCK

Potlucks are social events where each attendee brings a dish to share. They can be held at a workplace, community center, or someone's home, and are a fun and affordable way to gather and try new foods.   My idea of a good Potluck dish is something homemade, delicious that can easily be transported - and gluten-free.

Since attending Potlucks can be a nightmare for someone gluten intolerant, I have tried to provide recipes that could be satisfying if it is the only item available at the event. Even if there are other gluten-free dishes, they may not be prepared safely. We have left many potlucks where although they had dishes marked gluten-free, there was nothing considered safe to eat.

Therefore, no matter what you make, I suggest you clearly mark your dish as gluten-free and also print off a message similar to what you will find in the Appendix (page 165) of "What to tell your guests".

Looking for the perfect gluten-free lasagna recipe? Look no further! This classic dish is a staple in any home cook's repertoire and for good reason. It has layers of pasta, meat and/or vegetables, and cheese all baked together in a savory tomato sauce that is sure to please more than just your gluten-free guests.

This recipe has a few shortcut ingredients that make it gluten-free, but still have a ton of flavor. It's a family favorite that nobody will guess is gluten-free!

 **Prep**
30 Mins

 **Cook Time**
60 Mins

 **Serves**
10-12

 **Difficulty**
Medium

Ingredients

1 box (about 10 oz or 250 g) of gluten-free oven ready lasagna noodles

2 cups (450 g) shredded mozzarella cheese

Small container (8 oz or 225 g) ricotta cheese

1/2 block of cream cheese (4 oz or 125 g) - softened

1/2 cup (45 g) grated parmesan cheese

2 large eggs

1/2 onion, finely diced

29 oz (680 ml) can of tomato sauce

25 oz (680 g) pasta sauce

1 lb (450 g) ground/minced beef

Salt and Pepper

Cooking brings people together!

Special Supplies

- a 9"x 13" (23cm x 33cm) baking pan with high sides. I suggest a disposable aluminum/aluminium/ pan be used if transporting to avoid cleaning or worry that your pan may be broken.
- Gluten-free lasagna noodles are pretty common in your local grocery stores. It is much easier to use the oven-ready type. They can be found alongside regular pasta or also found in the Organic/Gluten free section of the store.
- Although normally I recommend pasta with more than one gluten-free flour blend, as these are cooked within a casserole rather than boiled, any gluten-free lasagna noodles that are oven-ready are the best.

Gluten Precautions

- Please ensure your baking pan is clean. Using parchment paper doesn't work in this recipe. You can try to form aluminum foil around and up the sides of your pan to be extra careful. As mentioned above, a disposable aluminum/aluminium pan is easy to use, and even easier to clean up.

- Please clean and check you skillet well. Do NOT use a skillet if it has any scratches or large marks where gluten can hide.

- Obviously, the lasagna noodles need to be made gluten-free, but also check your pasta sauce and spices. Although I believe it has been proven to be a myth, I would verify that if you select pre-shredded cheese, that they don't use any gluten containing products to prevent clumping. I have seen some use potato starch but never flour, but I would suggest you still check.

- The dish is cooked covered for most of the time, but please ensure it is cooked in a non-convection oven or without the convection setting as we don't want the air circulating while this bakes when it is not covered.

- Please carefully clean your can opener prior to use.

- Cheese graters commonly have many places for gluten to hide. Please ensure it is cleaned carefully before use with a brush.

Directions

STEP 1

Preheat oven to **425°F (220°C).**

Set aside 1 cup of the mozzarella cheese for topping the lasagna when it is nearly done. In a medium bowl, mix the remaining mozzarella, ricotta, cream cheese, parmesan, and eggs. Add a sprinkle of salt and pepper. Set aside.

STEP 2

In a large skillet over medium-high heat, add the ground/minced beef and onion. Brown the beef, breaking it into very small chunks until cooked through.

STEP 3

Drain the meat of any excess grease and return to the pan. Add the sauces and mix until heated through.

STEP 4

Spoon a thin layer of sauce onto the bottom of your baking dish. Using 5 noodles for the first layer – dip each noodle in the sauce and then lay that noodle in the pan covering the bottom. You can break any noodle to ensure it fits in the pan. Don't worry if a noodle breaks accidentally, just layer it in the best you can! Make sure the layer of noodles is covered with a layer of sauce.

Add half the cheese mixture across the noodle base. You can spread it with a spatula to smooth it. Add some more sauce over the cheese layer. You should have used about 1/3 of your sauce.

STEP 5

Do another layer of about 5 noodles ensuring to dip them in sauce and then lay in dish. Add the other half of cheese mixture in dollops and spread to smooth. Add more sauce over cheese layer. This should use another 1/3 of overall sauce.

Finally, dip the remining noodles in sauce and layer in dish and cover in any remaining sauce. This should use the final third of overall sauce.

STEP 6

Cover the dish tightly with aluminium foil and bake for 40 minutes covered.   Remove the foil and top with remaining mozzarella cheese and bake for another 15-20 minutes until it is browned and bubbling.

STEP 7

Let the lasagna sit for 20 minutes before serving. Slice and enjoy!

Notes

- You can use your choice of cheeses, even dairy free if you require. I prefer a mixture of cheddar and mozzarella.
    - You can use your choice of meat as well. Ground/Minced turkey, chicken or even sausage meat are all excellent choices.

Slow cookers are convenient and require minimal prep work making it easy to prepare a large quantity of food with little effort. This bean medley is a tasty combination of different beans, vegetables, and seasonings. Best of all, it can be customized to suit a wide range of tastes.

This truly is a hearty and flavorful gluten-free dish which is a perfect fit for a potluck event or even for a at home meal for the family..

 **Prep**
5 Mins

 **Cook Time**
5-6 hours

 **Serves**
10-12

 **Difficulty**
Easy

SLOW COOKER BEAN MEDLEY

Ingredients

1 1/2 cups (375 ml) ketchup

2 stalks celery, chopped

1 medium onion, chopped

1 medium green pepper, chopped

1 medium sweet red pepper, chopped

1/4 cup (50 g) packed brown sugar

1/2 cup (125 ml) water

1/2 cup (125 ml) Italian salad dressing

2 bay leaves (optional)

1 tablespoon (15 ml) cider vinegar

1 teaspoon ground mustard

1/8 teaspoon pepper

1 can (15 oz or 540 ml)) whole kernel corn, drained

1 can (16 oz or 540 ml) EACH kidney beans, black-eyed peas, great northern beans, lima beans, and black beans, all rinsed and drained

Special Supplies

- a clean 5 qt (5 L) slow cooker

Gluten Precautions

- Not normally a high source for cross-contact, but please carefully wipe the cutting edge on your can opener. If the last thing you opened contained gluten, then this can cross-contaminate the current cans you need to open.
- Some Italian salad dressings do contain a gluten source. Please verify your container in the fridge or at the store when purchasing.
- Please verify the beans and corn do not contain a 'may contain' gluten warning.
- Please carefully clean your can opener prior to use.
- Colanders and strainers are notoriously hard to clean and should be avoided. To drain your beans and/or corn, I suggest you check out my Tips chapter on page 38, for suggestions on doing this safely.
- Ketchup and mustard are more commonly found as a squeeze bottle but it is still possible for gluten crumbs to be sucked into the tip when the squeeze is released if tip is wiped on bread for example. Please buy or open a new bottle of each if there are any chance of crumbs.
- Many people use a piece of bread in their brown sugar container to keep it soft. Please ensure nothing is or was previously stored in this container to soften it.

Directions

STEP 1

In a 5-qt. slow cooker, combine everything but the beans and corn. Stir well then mix in the remaining ingredients. Cover and cook on low for 5-6 hours. If you used bay leaves, please ensure you discard before serving.

Notes

- Feel free to change up the beans to your favorites or what you may have on hand.

Tater tot casserole is a hearty and comforting dish that is sure to be a favorite. With a savory meat base and vegetables, topped with a layer of crispy tater tots, this casserole is the perfect blend of flavors and textures.
And the best part? It's a snap to prepare gluten-free!

This taco-inspired tater tot casserole recipe is packed with black beans, corn, cheese, ground/minced beef, and a whole lot of flavor.

MEXICAN TATER TOT CASSEROLE

 **Prep**
25 Mins

 **Cook Time**
45 Mins

 **Serves**
8

 **Difficulty**
Easy

Ingredients

1 bag (2 lbs or 800g) frozen tater tots (about 4 cups)

3 cups (750 ml) cheese, shredded - I like a mix of mozzarella and cheddar

1 lb (450 g) ground/minced beef

1/4 cup (60 ml) onion - finely diced

1 packet (1 oz or 28 g) taco seasoning (gluten-free) or mix spices as described in Gluten Precaution area

1 can (4 oz or 127 ml) green chilies

1 can (15 oz - 540 ml) black beans - drained

14 oz or 400 g frozen corn - about 3 cups

1 small can (10 oz or 300 ml) red enchilada sauce, just over a cup

Salt and Pepper

Embrace the challenge.

Special Supplies

- a 9"x 13" (23cm x 33cm) baking pan with high sides.
- Tater tots that are gluten-free can be found in your local grocery stores. A few brands and flavors MAY contain gluten though so please check ingredients carefully.

Gluten Precautions

- Please ensure your baking pan is clean. You can try to form aluminum/aluminium foil around and up the sides of your pan to be extra careful. If just using a plain pan, you may want to spray with a verified spray that doesn't contain gluten to make cleanup easier. Even better, I suggest a disposable aluminum baking tray.
- Please clean and check your skillet well. Do NOT use a skillet if it has any scratches or large marks where gluten can hide.
- Carefully watch your taco seasoning as some contain gluten. If you cannot find a packaged gluten-free taco seasoning - mix 1 Tbsp chili powder, 1 1/2 tsp ground cumin, 1 tsp sea salt, 1 tsp ground black pepper, 1 tsp ground paprika, 1/4 tsp garlic powder, 1/4 tsp onion powder, 1/4 tsp crushed red pepper flakes and 1/4 tsp dried oregano.
- Don't forget to verify the enchilada sauce is gluten-free. Carefully use the Reading Labels chapter to ensure there is no gluten.
- Spices are used a lot in all types of cooking, but many are processed in facilities where gluten exists. Although they don't 'contain' gluten, please watch for 'may contain' statements on ALL your spices.
- Colanders and strainers are notoriously hard to clean and should be avoided. To drain your beans and/or lentils, I suggest you check out my Tips chapter on page 38, for suggestions on doing this safely.
- Please carefully clean your can opener prior to use.

Directions

STEP 1

Preheat Oven to **375°F (190°C).**

Add the ground/minced beef and the onion to a clean 12-inch skillet, brown meat until thoroughly cooked. Drain off excess fat and return to skillet.

STEP 2

Add the taco seasoning, green chiles, black beans, frozen corn, and the enchilada sauce to the meat and onion, and stir until combined. Cook for an additional 8-10 minutes over medium heat.

STEP 3

Add 2 cups of shredded cheese to the meat mixture and stir until blended. Pour into the baking dish and spread evenly around.

STEP 4

Place the frozen tater tots evenly over the top. Bake for 35 to 40 minutes.

STEP 5

Remove from oven, add the remaining cup of cheese over the top. Bake another 5 minutes or until cheese is melted.

Notes

- Ground/Minced pork or sausage meat is an excellent substitute for the beef.
- If you don't like black beans, change them up. Feel free to add other favorites. I like to add canned mushrooms sometimes.

A seven-layer salad is a refreshing and flavorful dish that is perfect for any occasion. With layers of crisp lettuce, vegetables, and a variety of tasty toppings, this salad is as delicious as it is visually appealing. The best part? It's easy to customize with your favorite ingredients, making it a versatile choice for any palate. Need vegetarian, leave off the bacon.

Give this recipe a try and discover why it's a classic favorite! It's a beautiful dish to look at if you have a fancy glass dish but can be equally impressive in just a glass 9x13 pan.

SEVEN LAYER SALAD

 **Prep**
20 Mins

 **Cook Time**
15 Mins

 **Serves**
6-8

 **Difficulty**
Easy

Ingredients

4 large eggs

1 small head iceberg lettuce, chopped

1 cup (250 ml) cherry tomatoes, halved

1 (16 oz - 750 g) package frozen green peas, defrosted

1 cup cucumbers, chopped

1 red onion, chopped

1 1/2 cups (375 ml) mayonnaise

2 teaspoons (10 ml) sugar

1 teaspoon seasoned salt

1/4 teaspoon garlic powder

1/2 lb (250 g) bacon, cooked and crumbled

Special Supplies

- A beautiful, glass trifle dish will show the layers of this salad perfectly, but most will not have this sort of dish. I have made this many times in a casserole dish or a 9"x13" (23cm x 33cm) glass dish. I do think it presents better in something glass allowing you to see the layers. Just make sure it is perfectly clean.

Gluten Precautions

- Please clean your serving dish and cooking pot and utensils well.
- Sometimes wheat can be added as a binder in bacon. Usually, you can easily find the ones that are safe if you verify the ingredients label.
- Spices are used a lot in all types of cooking but many are processed in facilities where gluten exists. Although they don't 'contain' gluten, please watch for 'may contain' statements on ALL your spices.
- Mayonnaise is normally gluten-free and it can be found in both a jar and a squeeze bottle. However, it is commonly used for bread so a new jar or bottle is preferred as a gluteny knife can be dipped a long way into the jar so you can't simply remove the top portion. As well, if the tip of a squeeze bottle has been wiped on bread, gluten crumbs can then be sucked back into bottle when sides are released, contaminating it with gluten. If you are 100% sure the tip is safe, then you can use it.

Directions

STEP 1

Place the eggs in a medium saucepan and ensure they are covered with water. Bring to a boil on the stovetop. Cover, remove from the heat, and let sit for 12 minutes.

While the eggs are cooking, place some ice into a medium-sized bowl of water. Once the eggs are done cooking, add them to the bowl of iced water and let them cool for 10 minutes as you move on to the next step.

STEP 2

In a medium bowl, whisk together the mayonnaise, sugar, seasoned salt, and garlic powder. Set aside. Peel and chop the eggs.

STEP 3

In your choice of serving dish, layer the lettuce, red onion, tomatoes, cucumber and peas. Top with the mayonnaise mixture, then the hard boiled eggs and bacon. Serve.

STEP 4

If you are not serving this right away, please leave the the eggs and bacon off until ready to serve.

Notes

- Ensure you cut all the vegetables a reasonable size so it is easier to serve and looks nice when finished.
- This salad can be served right away or you can make it up to 24 hours in advance. If you are making it in advance, omit the egg and bacon and add them right before serving. Refrigerate.
- It's important that if you are not serving the salad right away to keep the order of the layers the same. Mixing them up can result in a soggy salad. I would suggest you ensure that the dressing sits on top of the peas as these won't become soggy. If you can do this the salad can sit (refrigerated) for 24 hours before serving.
  - Feel free to substitute ANY of the vegetables. Broccoli florets, cauliflower florets or even shredded carrots are excellent. Adding some shredded cheddar to the top is something I almost always add too.

DESSERTS

Why do I feel this will be the most popular chapter? Desserts are normally a highly anticipated aspect of any meal. It's the indulgence you probably shouldn't have, but most people will gladly eat when offered. If you're going to be bad, let's make sure it's really good.

I have included some recipes on the following pages that are easy to prepare and delicious, but let's not forget the ease of buying something **premade**. Especially at a large group dinner sometimes buying a dessert will help you keep your sanity to survive the event.

Most grocery stores have premade **gluten-free cakes and pies**. Remember to look in the regular dessert section as well as the Gluten Free/Organic section of grocery stores and don't forget to check the freezer areas for frozen options. Many gluten-free products are kept frozen. Just always check ingredients as many items in these sections are not all gluten-free as stores sometimes fill space in a freezer marked gluten-free with non gluten-free items. Not everything Organic is gluten-free.

You can find really good options at **Farmer's Markets** or **Specialty stores** as well.

Most grocery stores have **premade gluten-free pie crusts** and you can just fill them with your choice of a gluten-free filling. Check any canned pie fillings as sometimes they are thickened with flour. You can make your own or look in the gluten-free section of the store or go to a Natural food store to find a good filling.

**Ice cream** is always a good choice. True, high quality plain ice cream is usually gluten-free, but many kinds are made unsafe due to the flavorings. Usually vanilla is a safe choice, but don't rule out other more exciting flavors, and never assume a flavor does or doesn't have gluten. Always read the label.

Another excellent option is **Pudding** or a **Gelatin** dessert. Regular flavored gelatin and most puddings are gluten-free. Always read the label.

There are many pre-packaged gluten-free baking mixes - **Cakes, Quick Bread,** Slices. They may not be premade, but are simple to pull together and can be made in advance.

**Whipping cream** is gluten-free. Just buy a heavy whipping cream and whip away with appropriate flavors and sweeteners. Also, consider frozen tubs of whipped desserts like Cool Whip and even pressurized whipped topping containers. Most are gluten-free. Always read the label.

Did you know that most premade **frostings/icings** are gluten-free? As always, check the ingredients.

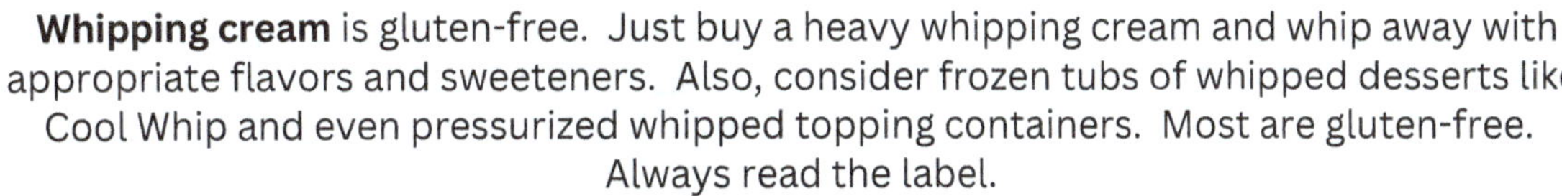

SSERTS

PUDDING CUPCAKES
(AKA Fairy Cakes)

This boxed cake mix plus pudding recipe has been around forever, but has been updated now to meet the growing number of gluten-intolerant people. The taste is amazing and hard to believe you just dump a few packages into a bowl, mix and then bake.

It's so easy to change the toppings each time to make them unique.

These treats are also free from nuts (aside from pistachio flavor) so are a good choice for a school event.

 **Prep**
10 Mins

 **Cook Time**
20 Mins

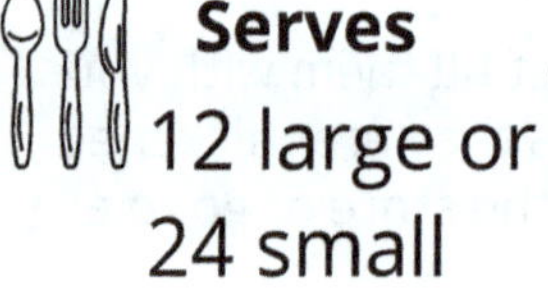 **Serves**
12 large or
24 small

 **Difficulty**
Easy

Ingredients

1 package gluten-free cake mix - golden, yellow, white or even chocolate

1 instant pudding box - your choice flavor Vanilla, Chocolate, Banana, Pistachio etc. (3.4 oz or 99 g)

1 cup (250 ml) milk
4 large eggs
1/3 cup (80 ml) vegetable oil

Frosting or whipped topping as desired. (as shown in picture)

Happiness never decreases by being shared!

Special Supplies

- paper cupcake liners/cases (12 or 24)
- You will need one or two - 12 hole, clean muffin tins.
- Gluten-free cake mixes can usually be found alongside the regular cake mixes. They can also be found in the Organic and Gluten Free sections of your store.

Gluten Precautions

- There is no real need for a stand or hand mixer in this case. It is a thick batter but manageable with a sturdy spoon or whisk. If you choose to use a mixer, please ensure there are no residues especially in areas not easily visible and disclose that a mixer was used to the recipient.
- Although these are baked in cupcake liners/cases, it is possible that cupcakes will rise up over the tops of the liners. Therefore, please ensure your muffin tin is cleaned well prior to use.
- Ensure these are baked in a non-convection oven as we don't want the air circulating while these bake.
- Most pudding mixes are gluten-free, but please read the label.
- Metal cooling racks are notoriously hard to clean and should normally be avoided. In this case however, the liners/cases should protect the cupcake from any cross-contact.

Directions

STEP 1

Preheat oven to **350°F (177°C)**

Combine all the ingredients in a bowl with a clean whisk. Make sure you add cake mix and pudding mix as is and don't follow instructions on packaging.

STEP 2

Blend slowly until combined, then mix vigorously for a few minutes until well blended.

STEP 3

Pour into either 12 muffin tins lined with paper cups right to the top of the paper lining (for large cupcakes) OR fill 24 liners about 1/2 full (for smaller cupcakes). Bake for about 30 minutes for the larger ones or 20 minutes for smaller until a toothpick stick in centre of cupcake comes out clean.

STEP 4

Remove cupcakes from muffin pan and cool completely on cooling rack. Frost or decorate as desired.

Notes

- My favorite combination is a golden cake mix with pistachio pudding mix. Let your tastes be creative.
- Please use your creativity to think of new additives to the batter but be aware any additives could effect cooking time and as always, ensure they are gluten-free.
- If you only have 1 muffin tin but want to make 24, just bake the first 12 while the extra batter sits. Then after you take the first 12 cupcakes out, use 12 new liners/cases and fill the remaining 12 cupcakes. Be careful as pan will be hot and they may cook a little quicker.
- Ensure you store finished items in an airtight container away from contaminates until ready to serve.

I'm not sure why this dessert isn't more popular in today's world. It is a tasty and visually appealing treat that is sure to impress. It is also naturally gluten-free and only has a few easy ingredients. Despite being named after the Russian ballerina, these are considered more an Australian dessert than Russian.

It has a wonderful meringue crust on the outside while the center is like a soft marshmallow and is usually topped with whipping cream and whatever your favorite or in-season fruit is available. This is one of those desserts that steals the show.

 **Prep**
30 Mins

 **Cook Time**
1 hr, 45 min

 **Serves**
12-16

 **Difficulty**
Medium

Ingredients

6 large egg whites - room temperature

1 1/2 cups (300 g) granulated sugar

2 teaspoon (10 ml) cornstarch*

1/2 teaspoon vanilla

1/2 teaspoon lemon juice

1 1/2 cups (375 ml) heavy or whipping cream (very cold)

2 tablespoons (30 ml) granulated sugar

4-5 cups (1000-1250 ml) fresh fruit of choice - sliced berries, kiwi, blueberries, peaches, raspberries, etc

* In the UK and Australia, please use Cornflour

The kitchen is your playground!

Special Supplies

- parchment paper
- 2 clean baking sheets
- piping bag or a large storage or freezer bag

Gluten Precautions

- Using parchment paper on your baking sheet will prevent contact with whatever may have been previously made on this same baking sheet. In addition it makes it easier and safer to remove the pavlovas.

- The safest way to whip the egg whites is by hand, but this is unrealistic in this case due to the amount of whipping necessary. I think it is necessary to use your stand mixer or hand mixer and the whisk attachment regardless of which mixer is used. However, please ensure that the entire mixer and whisk attachment are clean including the area where the whisk attaches to the unit. Suggest using a small brush to get in where it is hard to just wipe and is easy for gluten to hide like the holes where the beaters go and the tiny spaces of the whisk where it comes together at the top and bottom.

- Ensure these are baked in a non-convection oven as we don't want the air circulating while they bake.

Notes

- Ensure there are NO yolks when separating your eggs. Even the tiniest amount will ruin your pavlovas. This is one time older eggs are better than fresh eggs.

- Although the egg whites will whip up better when they are not cold, they are easier to separate when they are cold. I suggest you separate them cold from the fridge, but then let whites sit at room temp for a while (or you can place the bowl of whites in warm water).

- Although the pavlovas can be made about 3 days in advance, they should not be topped until right before serving. Once the whipping cream and fruit are applied, the pavlovas will start to soften immediately and should be consumed right away.

- It is important that once the mixture is done whipping that the nests are formed and put into the preheated oven within 5-10 minutes as they will slowly deflate. They don't have to look perfect and when served will be covered with whipping cream and fruit so don't worry about perfection.

- Ensure you store finished items in an airtight container away from contaminates until ready to serve. Be careful as they are delicate.

- Do not place these in the fridge or freezer. If they get cold they will perspire when they warm up/thaw which will cause them to get wet and soggy.

Directions

STEP 1

Preheat oven to **225° F (107°C)**

Line 2 clean baking sheets with parchment paper. (Optional - Draw eight - 3 inch (8 cm) circles on each piece of parchment paper spacing them out evenly. Then turn the parchment paper over to hide pen/pencil marks, but you can still see the lines.)

STEP 2

Using your mixer of choice, beat the 6 egg whites on high speed for 1 minute until soft peaks form. With the mixer still going, gradually add the 1 1/2 c of sugar and then beat for 10 min on high speed, or until stiff peaks form. If you turn the whisk to face up, it should have a stiff peak. It will be smooth and glossy.

STEP 3

Using a clean spatula, quickly fold in the lemon juice and vanilla extract. Then fold in the corn starch and mix until well blended.

STEP 4

You'll want to form 6-8 nests that are 3" (8 cm) in diameter and slightly raised onto the parchment paper of each baking sheet (for a total of 12-16 pavlovas). This is where the circles you may have drawn in step one come in handy. You can form these circles using spoons, patience, and skill, OR maybe a piping bag. I find it easiest to just place the mixture in a plastic Ziploc type storage or freezer bag. (If you place the bag in a small bowl with the top sides folded over the rim of the bowl and then use a spatula to scoop the mixture into the bag, it goes quickly). You can always refill this bag if necessary. Then squeeze the mixture to one corner of the bag and cut a small diagonal 1/4" piece of this corner off. Gentle squeeze the egg mixture out forming a complete circle and continue to pipe around the circle and up a bit to form a little nest-like mound. Then using a spoon, indent the center to allow room for cream and fruit when cooked.

STEP 5

Bake for 1 hour and 15 min then turn the oven off and <u>without opening</u> the door, let them sit in the hot oven another 30 min. The outsides of pavlova will be dry and crisp if you tap it and very pale. Don't worry the insides will still be marshmallow soft.

STEP 6

Beat the cold whipping cream with 2 tbsps sugar in a cold bowl for 2 to 2 1/2 minutes or until whipped and spreadable.

Also ensure you prepare the fruit. You want the fruit easy to scoop onto pavlovas. You'll want to slice larger fruit.

Suggest you get both of these ready to go but stop here until you are ready to serve.

STEP 7

Right before you are ready to serve, spread or pipe the frosting onto each pavlova nest and then top it with fresh fruit.

Cheesecake......gluten-free.......what???

Cheesecake bars are a delicious and creamy dessert that combines the rich flavor of cheesecake with the convenience of a bar. This cheesecake is flavorful and unlikely anyone would realize there was no gluten in the crust. The only real difference between this and a traditional cheesecake is this is not baked in a springform pan. It is one pan that is hard to use for gluten-free once it's been used for gluten, therefore we are going to avoid it altogether.

These rich and indulgent bars are a perfect dessert for any occasion and are sure to satisfy your sweet tooth.

 **Prep**
15 Mins
(plus chilling time)

 **Cook Time**
45 min

 **Serves**
18

 **Difficulty**
Easy

Ingredients

<u>Filling</u>

- 4 blocks (32 oz or 1 kg) cream cheese, room temperature
- 1 cup (200 g) granulated sugar
- 1/2 cup (125 ml) sour cream
- 2 teaspoons (10 ml) vanilla
- 4 large eggs room temp, slightly beaten

<u>Crust</u>

- 3 cups (750 ml) of crumbs - cookie/biscuit (graham, outside of Oreo-like cookie, etc), cereal, pretzels, etc., that are gluten-free
- 1/2 cup (100 g) sugar
- 12 tablespoons (1 1/2 sticks) 168 g unsalted butter - melted
- Fruit topping of your own choice or a gluten-free verified bottled sauce like caramel, chocolate, or strawberry

CHEESECAKE BARS

Special Supplies

- Aluminum/Aluminium foil or parchment paper
- 9"x 13" (23cm x 33cm) pan

Gluten Precautions

- Unfortunately, unless you have a new springform pan, it would be difficult to ensure it is free from gluten as you can't complete a barrier for the crust and there are lots of places gluten can hide. This pan would be considered high-risk due to what it normally would be used to bake. Therefore, this recipe offers some tips to cook in a rectangular pan, while still maintaining great taste and texture.

- Parchment paper, however, does work well in a rectangular pan. It isn't needed if the pan is clean, but always provides a good barrier and makes it easier to remove and cut. Please see Tips for using Parchment paper in the Appendix (pg 166-167)

- Creaming the cream cheese is much easier with a stand or hand mixer. However, please ensure that the entire mixer is clean including the area where the beaters attach to the unit. I suggest using a small brush to get in where it is hard to just wipe and is easy for gluten to hide like the holes where the beaters attach.

- Ensure it is baked in a non convection oven as we don't want the air circulating while this bakes.

- Butter/Margarine is a common source of cross-contact issues. Please be careful to ensure there are no crumb particles.

- If you use a blender to create your crumbs, please ensure you clean the blender well including running the blender with water and a few drops of dish soap to better clean where the blades turn. These are hard areas to clean and could hide residual gluten from a previous food item.

Directions

STEP 1

Preheat oven to **325° F (165°C)**. Spray with a gluten-free spray or line your baking dish with aluminum/aluminium foil or parchment paper.

STEP 2

Mix the choice of crumbs, sugar and melted butter together then press it into the baking dish in an even layer.

STEP 3

Using your clean hand or stand mixer, add the cream cheese and sugar and beat on high speed until light and fluffy. Lower the speed to medium and add in the eggs one at a time, then sour cream and vanilla, and blend until smooth.

STEP 4

Carefully spread mixture on the crust and bake for 40-45 minutes, until set and firm.

STEP 5

Chill completely before serving. Serve plain or feel free to add whipping cream, fresh fruit, or some sort of squeeze bottle topping sauce like strawberry, chocolate, or caramel

Notes

- Ensure you store finished cheesecake in a sealed container in refrigerator away from contaminates until ready to serve. Can be stored up to a week.
- If using a crust option that is less sweet like pretzels, you may want to increase sugar slightly.
- The cheese cake will taste better if brought back to room temperature before serving.
  - Think outside the box. My cheesecake crust in the picture was made from half gluten-free Oreos and Honey Nut Chex and tasted great.

Once again, delicious doesn't always mean difficult. This strawberry mousse is light, airy, and quite impressive-looking and only takes minutes to make (Although it does require a couple of hours to set after making it).

I usually serve this dessert in small bowls, but they can easily be made even more impressive with some sort of glassware. Let your creative side make this unique and don't forget to serve it with a dollop of whipped cream and a sprinkle of fresh strawberry slices for a refreshing and fruity dessert.

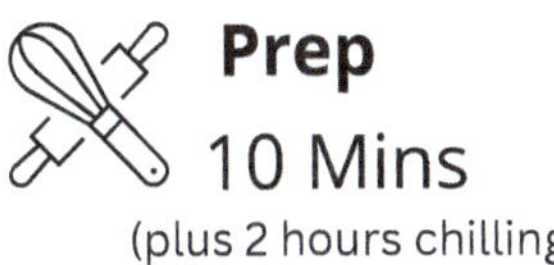 **Prep**
10 Mins
(plus 2 hours chilling)

 **Cook Time**
None

 **Serves**
4-6

 **Difficulty**
Easy

STRAWBERRY MOUSSE

Ingredients

3/4 cup (175 ml) boiling water

1 cup (250 ml) of ice cubes

1 package (0.3 oz or 85 g) strawberry gelatin mix

2 cups (500 ml) thawed whipped topping, divided*

2 cups (500 ml) strawberries, diced

* Whipped topping is NOT the same as whipping cream. If you cannot find frozen whipped topping, please see the Special Supplies section on page 92, for homemade whipped topping instructions.

Don't let fear stop you.

Special Supplies

- 4-6 individual serving dishes or bowls.

Gluten Precautions

- As always, check ingredients label of gelatin and whipped topping to ensure its gluten-free.

- Ensure all utensils and serving dishes are clean.

Directions

STEP 1

Place the strawberry gelatin into a large bowl. (I like to use a glass, 2-cup measuring cup as it makes adding ice cubes easier). Pour the boiling water into the bowl and stir until the gelatin mix has completely dissolved.

STEP 2

Add 1 cup (250 ml) of ice to the bowl. If you used the 2-cup glass measuring cup in Step 1, just drop ice cubes in the gelatin mix until the liquid reads 1 3/4 cups (425 ml). Stir until it's completely dissolved.

STEP 3

Gently stir in 1 1/2 cups (375 ml) of the whipped topping. The topping will get very liquidy, but keep stirring gently until no lumps remain.

STEP 4

When the whipped topping is blended in well, fold 1 1/2 cups (375 ml) of the diced fresh strawberries into the mixture. Be gentle. Spoon the mixture into dessert dishes and refrigerate for at least 2 hours.

STEP 5

Before serving, top the serving dishes with the remaining 1/2 cup of whipped topping and 1/2 cup of diced strawberries.

Notes

- Feel free to be creative in choice of your serving dish. I have used wine glasses (not really good for kids as they can easily tip over) or any clear glass. They do not all have to be the same.

- This can be made using sugar-free gelatin and whipped topping if desired.

This recipe only has a few ingredients, but the results will have your gluten-free guests amazed.

There are many different ways to mix up the flavors by changing the fruit. You can experiment with all the delicious variations that dump cakes have to offer!

Please note that although we call this a cake, it is more like a cobbler. It is scooped out with a spoon, not cut into pieces.

 **Prep**
5 Mins

 **Cook Time**
60 Mins

 **Serves**
12

 **Difficulty**
Super Easy

Ingredients

1 box gluten-free yellow or white cake mix

2 cans of pie filling - any flavor you like such as cherry, peaches, apples, etc. but ensure there is no gluten. - Feel free to mix 2 different flavors or maybe 1 can of pie filling mixed with a can of fruit like pineapple.

1 1/2 sticks (12 tablespoons or 168 grams) butter

DUMP CAKE

Be creative, be delicious!

Special Supplies

- a 9"x 13" (23cm x 33cm) pan - glass or metal but ensure it is cleaned well prior to use.

Gluten Precautions

- This recipe is super easy to ensure it's gluten-free. There is no mixer to worry about and only one dish to ensure is clean. The biggest concern with gluten will be to ensure your cake mix and pie filling or canned fruit is gluten-free.
- If you are using a spray to grease your pan please ensure it is gluten-free as well. Most regular sprays do not have gluten but there are a few that are meant for baking and include flour to prevent sticking. Avoid using these.
- Ensure this is cooked in a non-convection oven.
- Butter/Margarine is a common source of cross-contact issues. Please be careful to ensure there are no crumb particles.

Directions

STEP 1
Preheat the oven to **350°F (177°C).** Grease a clean 9"x 13" (23cm x 33cm) pan.

STEP 2
In your baking pan, dump your choice of canned pie fillings or fruit. Spread it around the bottom of pan evenly. If using 2 different types of fruit, feel free to mix them together or place half on one side and half on the other just ensure the thickness is even across the bottom of the pan.

STEP 3
Sprinkle the gluten-free cake mix evenly over the fruit bottom. Try to sprinkle as evenly as possible. There is no need to mix it in, in fact most say it doesn't turn out as well. Just sprinkle as evenly as possible.

STEP 4
Lastly, slice the butter into thin slices about 1/2 Tablespoon each so you have around 24 pieces. Then place the slices on the pan about 6 long and 4 across. You want the butter as evenly distributed along the top as possible.

STEP 5
Place in the preheated oven and bake for 45-60 minutes until nicely browned and bubbling. It's normal to see some wet spots on the top.

STEP 6
Allow it to cool slightly but this is best served warm. Once cool, refrigerate any leftovers. If you have any.

Notes

- If you are opening pie filling or canned fruit, please carefully clean your can opener prior to use.
- If you are using fresh or canned fruit, you will need to add liquid. I suggest you drain any liquid from the can and add enough water to make 1/2 cup total. Also, sprinkle about 1/2 cup of sugar over the fruit.
- If you feel creative, try other cake flavors like maybe chocolate, or consider adding nuts. Just think about what combinations sound good and make sure they are gluten-free.
- Feel free to make this at home then cover it in foil and you can reheat it at your destination.

146 • This is excellent with whipped cream or ice cream which melts wonderfully when warm.

DRINKS

It's hard to believe that even drinks can cause a problem for someone avoiding gluten, but it can. Luckily many drinks in general are gluten-free.

- **Water** – whether tap, mineral, or flavored, there is no gluten in pure water and we should all be drinking more.

- Pure fruit **juice and ciders** (non-alcoholic) have no gluten.

- **Smoothies** are usually just fruit juice and yogurt, but they sometimes have other ingredients. Please check to be sure there are no gluten ingredients added.

- Plain **milk**/creams are gluten-free. Additives like flavorings may contain gluten. Nut kinds of milk are generally OK, but Oat milk should state gluten-free due to cross-contact potential. Please read the packaging.

- Many **probiotic drinks** are gluten-free. Some though have cross-contact risks and barley malt and should be avoided.

- Plain black, green, white, oolong, and rooibos **teas** are gluten-free provided they do not contain any added flavorings or other ingredients.

- Plain **coffee** is gluten-free, but be careful to check the labels of all flavorings and additives. Also, be careful of premade coffee beverages as well. Check labels.

- **Chocolate drinks**: pure cocoa powder is gluten-free, but check things like chocolate milk and hot chocolate as some can contain gluten.

- Most brand-name **carbonated/fizzy drinks - sodas/pop** are gluten-free. For example Coca-Cola, Pepsi, 7-up, Sprite, Fresca, Fanta, and Mountain Due. Be wary of store brand names unless they state gluten-free or have completely safe ingredient labels.

- Avoid **malted drinks** - as malt is normally derived from barley.

- **Cider, sherry, port, and pure liqueurs** are gluten-free. Again though added flavorings may contain gluten.

- Unflavored **wines** should be gluten-free, whether still, fizzy, sweet, or dry.

- Spirits (vodka, tequila, gin, rum, whisky, and bourbon) are gluten-free as long as no gluten-containing product is added after distillation like some flavorings.

- Be careful of **cocktails,** which may have a gluten-containing product in them.

- Most **beer, lager, stout, and, ale** contain gluten. Avoid these.

- There is a growing range of **gluten-free beers** of all varieties available. There are two main types: <u>Gluten-Free Beers</u> which are made using gluten-free grains and <u>Gluten-Removed Beers</u>, which are made traditionally with barley and wheat, but then gluten is removed afterward. Gluten-free beers are a better choice for serving as some people do still react to gluten-removed beers.

- **Champagne** and **pure hard (alcoholic) ciders** are naturally gluten-free but as with other alcohols be on the lookout for other additives or flavorings that may contain gluten.

- **Coolers and other wine-flavored drinks** often have barley malt extract and are therefore unsafe. If it has an ingredient label, please check.

- According to the FDA in most countries, **all distilled alcohol is gluten-free**, unless gluten is added after distillation. However, some gluten-intolerant people state they can still react to them. I stand behind the Celiac Association's recommendations that these are safe.

This drink is delicious any time of the year, but I make it more commonly in the summertime.

It's simply a combination of tea and flavor and is super easy to make with cold-brew tea bags.   No boiling or waiting for it to cool. Simply mix ingredients, garnish, and serve!

It is also super easy to kick it up a notch by adding whiskey to a glass before adding the Ice Tea.

Just be careful when adding the alcohol as it is really easy to finish your glass quickly.

Prep
5 Mins

Serves
8

Difficulty
Easy

Ingredients

2 cold brew iced tea bags
2 quarts (2 L) cold water
1/2 cup (100 g) granulated sugar - optional
11 oz (325 ml) peach nectar
Ice
Optional
    1 1/2 oz honey Whiskey or regular Whiskey per glass

Sliced peaches

PEACH ICED TEA
(optional alcoholic version)

Cooking food well doesn't mean it has to be fancy.

Special Supplies

- Decorative serving glasses. I like a tall highball glass but any glass will suffice.
- A large - at least 2 Quart (2 Liter) Pitcher

Gluten Precautions

- This recipe is super easy to ensure it's gluten-free. Everything should be naturally gluten-free, but always read labels.
- I have never seen peach nectar that contains gluten, but please always check the label.
- If you are adding whiskey, just ensure you buy the basic flavors of Whiskey as sometimes gluten is added after distillation.

Directions

STEP 1

Add two cold brew tea bags to a 2 quart (2 L) pitcher of water. Allow to steep for 5 minutes, or longer if you prefer your iced tea stronger. Remove the tea bags and gently squeeze out excess, then discard.

STEP 2

Stir the sugar into the tea (if using), stirring until it dissolves. Add peach nectar to the tea and stir well.
Serve over ice. Garnish with fresh peach slices.

STEP 3 - OPTIONAL

For an alcoholic version simply add in 1 1/2 oz. of Whiskey and Ice to a tall glass. Fill the rest of the glass with iced tea. Enjoy!

Notes

- According to the FDA in most countries, <u>all distilled alcohol is gluten-free</u>, unless gluten is added after distillation. However, some gluten-intolerant people state they can still react to them. I stand behind the Celiac Association's recommendations that these are safe.

- If you can't find and don't have cold brew tea, you can still make this tea the traditional way. Simply brew your tea, cool it, then continue with the recipe.

  - Adding the nectar provides lots of sweetness. Feel free to leave out the sugar and add in only as much as necessary to meet your taste. You can even replace it with an artificial sweetener if desired.

This refreshing smoothie is the perfect way to start your day, relax after a day of work, refuel after a workout or sneak some vegetables into your child.

You choose the combination of fruit (and veggies if desired) and add some yogurt to create a delicious balance of flavors and creamy texture.

Simply blend all ingredients together and enjoy!

FRUIT SMOOTHIE

 **Prep**
5 Mins

 **Serves**
2

Difficulty
Easy

Ingredients

1/2 cup (125 ml) water, milk or juice

1 cup (250 ml) your favorite frozen fruit

1/2 cup (125 ml) plain yogurt (regular or Greek yogurt)

1 cup (250 ml) ice

Optional:
1/4 cup (60 ml) spinach, avocado, cauliflower OR zucchini

Suggestions:
- For frozen fruit use 1 cup of strawberries, blueberries, and raspberries plus a little spinach, and instead of plain, use vanilla-flavored yogurt.
- Try frozen mango for your fruit choice with vanilla yogurt.
- Replace 1 cup of fruit with 1 tbsp peanut butter and 2 bananas.
- Replace 1 cup of fruit with 1/2 cup spinach, 1/2 cup pineapple, and 1/4 cup orange juice or a tropical blend juice.

Follow your heart.

Special Supplies

- a well cleaned blender

Gluten Precautions

- The biggest concern with this recipe is your blender. It is hard to clean potential residual gluten from a blender due to the inaccessible parts underneath the moving blades. I suggest you place water with a couple of drops of dish soap in a blender and run for a few minutes. Dump the blender and rinse well. Then repeat once more.

- Plain yogurt is normally gluten-free. There are some flavors and brands that may contain gluten though so please check the label.

Directions

STEP 1

Place your choice of liquids in the clean blender.

STEP 2

Then add in frozen fruit, optional veggies, and yogurt. Place the lid on and blend for a few minutes until it is smooth. If using vegetables ensure it is blended longer to ensure the vegetables are not gritty.

STEP 3

Add the ice into the blender 1/2 cup (125 ml) at a time and blend between each addition until the smoothie is the consistency that you prefer. Serve immediately and enjoy!

Notes

- Try mixing flavors and feel free to add fresh fruit instead. Be aware though you may need extra ice to get the right consistency.
- Coconut water, coconut milk and almond milk all work wonderful in this recipe.
- Feel free to select a different gluten-free flavor of yogurt as well.
- Remember that if you add anything additional, please ensure it is gluten-free.

If you're looking for an easy non-alcoholic drink to share with friends and family, you should consider this fruit punch mocktail recipe. I have used this a few times at school events for the kids.

It is packed with fruit juice and adding the soda gives it a fizz which just makes it taste even better. It is very easy to adapt to what you may have on hand.

 **Prep**
5 Mins

 **Serves**
6

 **Difficulty**
Easy

MOCKTAIL (FRUIT PUNCH)

Ingredients

1 (64-ounce or 1.89 L) container cranberry juice cocktail

14 oz (400 ml) pineapple juice

1 container frozen lemonade

1 can lemon lime soda/fizzy (or ginger ale)

Orange slices (for garnish)

Fresh strawberries or cranberries (for garnish)

Lots of Ice

Optional - frozen fruit

Special Supplies

- a large glass punch bowl. Or you can use any large bowl that cannot easily be knocked over.

Gluten Precautions

- This recipe is super easy to ensure it's gluten-free. Just use basic juices and fruit. Never assume and always check labels.

Directions

STEP 1

Squeeze the container of frozen lemonade into a large drink or punch bowl.
Add the cranberry juice cocktail, pineapple juice, and fizzy drink/soda/pop. Gently stir to combine. Add plenty of ice.

STEP 2

Serve over ice and garnish with slices of oranges or any citrus and fresh berries.

Notes

- This punch can be easily adapted to what fruit or juices are available. I like to actually add frozen fruit to the bowl as it keeps the punch cold without diluting the taste.
- For a great addition, add a scoop of orange sherbet to each glass before pouring this delicious holiday punch!
- Want more fizz, simply add more lemon-lime or ginger ale soda.

LAST MINUTE IDEAS

It happens, your child forgets to tell you to bring a snack for school or you were planning to make something for work, but the date gets moved up and you no longer have time.

In addition to some things already mentioned in previous chapters, here are some quick things you can buy or make for those last minute demands.

- Buy some gluten-free **cookie/biscuits**. You do have to be careful as there are good and not-so-good gluten-free cookie/biscuits and gluten-free anything is not cheap. It is a personal taste obviously, but these are some of my favorites - chocolate chip ; gluten-free Oreos and similar type sandwich cookie/biscuits; macaroons, or macarons. Just remember my chapter on 'How to Read Labels', just because it should be gluten-free, doesn't mean it will be. Always read labels.

- **Ice cream** - obviously not a good choice to send to a school event or take to work, but plain ice cream is likely gluten-free and a good choice if someone is coming to your home. If you're buying a double chocolate brownie ice cream, you can guess it's likely not safe, but don't rule any out either. Some will surprise you. Check your freezer and look at the ingredients of what you have available.

- **Cheese Strings**. Another great last minute idea as many people already have these at home. Cheese strings are enjoyed by many people and not just kids. Just always read labels. If you want to have some fun, cut them into smaller pieces and put on a toothpick, and even better if you pair them with another choice like cucumber or a cherry tomato for a little cheese kebab..

- **Potato Chips/Crisps, Tortillas, Popcorn** - We all have these in our homes right? Most of these are gluten-free although they can be made unsafe with some of the flavors.

- Don't forget something healthy - **Fruit**. All pure fruit is gluten-free. Anything processed (dried, canned, roll-ups) needs to be checked. If you have fruit sitting in a fruit bowl exposed in your kitchen, there is a chance it could be covered in flour particles. As discussed in previous chapters, flour particles can float in the air and settle on things like a fruit bowl. Many laugh at this thought, but as we know it doesn't take much gluten to make someone sick. A simple rinse in the sink will remove any residual gluten that may have landed. Mix this with a fruit dip and you've got a great dish to serve.

COMPLETE DINNERS

Who doesn't enjoy being invited to a fancy dinner they don't have to cook themselves, especially a holiday dinner?

People who can't have gluten, that's who!

Many, many people dread the holidays simply because they know the household they are going to isn't gluten-free. It's not just a fear of being glutened either. It's also the fear of dealing with people that truly don't understand how dangerous it is to eat out. Many believe celiac isn't a real disease and heaven forbid you say you're gluten intolerant! And even if they believe it's real, they don't realize just how sick you can get from a little crumb.   It's frustrating to be looked at with eyes asking "Really? You're afraid of a crumb? Suck it up, it's not like it's an allergy and you can die!"

Gluten-intolerant people just want to enjoy the atmosphere with friends and family, but they don't want to be sick, judged or hurt the host's feelings. As stated in the Introduction (page 10), sharing a meal with others is more than just eating food. I know many families that have had family quarrels due to a gluten-intolerant guest refusing to eat food the host has prepared. This guest is not being overly dramatic though as there are so many areas that can turn a gluten-free food item unsafe it's scary. Sometimes cross-contact can occur from an unexpected guest's actions and the host is unaware it even happened.

As someone who has driven home from a gluten-free holiday dinner and regular family dinners that a close relative prepared with a lot of care and we are dealing with a young child throwing up in the back seat, it is not something you forget. The dinners were gluten-free, but my child's reaction tells me something went wrong. In one case we believe the culprit to be a spaghetti spoon stirring both regular and gluten-free pasta. The pasta was correctly cooked in different pots and the gluten-free pasta was strained first through a clean strainer, but my sister admitted the same spoon was used to stir both. In other cases, we have some ideas on what may have caused the problem, but we likely will never really know. It was obvious on our way home that something got through. Luckily, our daughter recovered with no hospital visits and it was only an uncomfortable situation for a few hours. Although we can't see permanent damage that may have occurred on the inside.

The thing to note is you often don't know where the cross-contact came from, but it is easy to happen at large dinners with multiple people especially when you have gluten-free and gluten dishes. The host can prepare the entire meal perfectly safe, but then one of the other guests may accidentally sprinkle regular bun crumbs over a gluten-free dish or dip their gluten item in the gluten-free dip and contaminate it without the knowledge of anyone else.

Most people can read a package and decide if a product has any gluten-containing ingredients. I have already shown you how to do this in the 'Reading Labels' chapter (pages 16-24) and this is just the first step. Ensuring a safe, gluten-free meal is A LOT more than just ensuring all the items have no gluten.   Many more steps are needed to make a holiday dinner safe.

Let's start by asking -
Is the dinner going to be 100% gluten-free?

OR

Is the dinner going to have both gluten-free and gluten items?

If there are NO gluten dishes it is easier to prevent cross-contact during the meal, but basic steps are still needed to prevent gluten cross-contact while preparing your dishes.

Most people that host a dinner will have both gluten-free AND gluten dishes to appeal to all guests that refuse to eat gluten-free as they think it can't be as delicious.

You know some of these people. You may be one of these people!

Therefore, my focus for the following pages will be on hosting a dinner that will include BOTH gluten-free and gluten items. HOWEVER, the instructions I provide will be for a **completely gluten-free meal**. This way you have everything you need to make it 100% gluten-free, but can decide for yourself what may not be gluten-free and take the steps necessary to make it safe and delicious for all. Maybe you even want others to bring a dish, but you can still ensure it is safe for your gluten-free guest.

Most gluten-free guests will still be happy to know there is safe food for them even if everything isn't gluten-free. Just please communicate with your gluten-avoiding guest.

ROAST BEEF DINNER

- If you're cooking a fully gluten-free meal you'll be buying things that will generally cost more, therefore I suggest you stick with just a good quality **Roast**. No need for the expensive prime rib, but it's completely your choice.

- For **potatoes**, I'm suggesting traditional mashed potatoes. My pick is Yukon Gold for the best result, but any potato you have available will work for mashed potatoes. Please see my recipe for mashed potatoes in the Side Dish chapter (page 111) and adjust for the number of people.

- For the first side, I recommend **carrots**. They are economical to buy any time of the year and easy to prepare and delicious.   Simply peel them, cut them into bite-sized pieces, and place them in a large, clean pot with water. Boil for about 30 minutes. (We like our carrots nice and soft so adjust to your taste) After they are cooked, drain and serve. I find it easiest to let your guests decide how to season them to their taste.

- For the second side dish, I propose a large **garden salad**. They are easy to make and with no cooking needed, it frees space in your kitchen. You can find some interesting salad dressings or even make your own, but do watch for gluten in some dressings. Anything with malt vinegar should be avoided. Read labels and place them on the table. Have a few varieties and let guests choose their favorite.

- If you're familiar with **gluten-free dinner buns/rolls**, just buy a package of good ones from your local grocer. However, please note that there are still ones that most people would consider equivalent to eating saw dust despite there being lots of great-tasting ones too. It varies widely from one celiac to another which they prefer. I don't think it is inappropriate to call your gluten-free guest and ask them for a suggestion of their favorite gluten-free buns. I do NOT suggest trying to make gluten-free buns/rolls yourself. Even for seasoned bakers, gluten-free bread baking isn't as simple as replacing all-purpose flour with gluten-free flour in your recipe.

- For an additional special side dish, I'm suggesting individual **Yorkshire puddings**. They are easy to make with only 3 ingredients. The biggest issue will be they take oven time which is always hard to plan. Please see my recipe in the Side Dish chapter (page 123) and follow these tips on how to include with this meal.

  Since Yorkshires are best served fresh, begin making these about 1 hour prior to the meal. I would make the batter first as these are better when the batter rests. Then proceed to get the empty muffin pan ready to go in the oven right as the roast is finishing cooking. You can place the pan with shortening only, into the oven with the roast about 20 minutes before the roast is done.

  When the Roast comes out of the oven, crank up the heat to 425°F (220°C). The pan can continue to heat to 425°F (220°C) while the roast sits for a short time for the juices to redistribute back into the meat before slicing. When the oven reaches this higher temperature, you can continue with the recipe in Step 3, to add batter to the hot pan and bake.

- **Gravy** - Since this is a roast meal with possible Yorkshires, you'll want lots of gravy. Gravy can be easily made gluten-free using either dripping from the roast pan, plus water, beef broth, or water drained from carrots or potatoes.

  You'll likely need 1/3-1/2 cup per person. Please see my recipe for gravy in the Side Dish chapter (page 108).

- As for the best part of the meal, you can look at my dessert chapter, but I stand behind considering buying a dessert since you'll already be doing a lot of work on the meal and ensuring everything is gluten-free. I would suggest buying a plain, gluten-free **Cheesecake** or making my Cheesecake Bar recipe (on page 141) and serving it with **Ice cream** for those that prefer.

  You can buy toppings in different flavors like caramel, strawberry, or chocolate that are gluten-free or maybe just some fresh fruit. Although there are always exceptions, usually, the only gluten in a cheesecake is in the crust but they are easy to make gluten-free yourself maybe a day in advance, and just let it sit in the fridge until needed.

- You'll need to think about drinks that can be served before the meal, during the meal, and after. For Christmas, I love the idea of **Eggnog**. It can be made alcoholic or not (Basic Brandy and Rum are gluten-free and you can check some spiced rums on the internet to ensure they are still gluten free after spices added). Even the kids can enjoy this one in non-alcohol form.   Another good option is a **punch** of some kind and guests can serve themselves. During the meal itself, a good **wine** is perfect. For a roast beef dinner you want a well-balanced, red wines like a Cabernet Sauvignon or Merlot. Afterward, get the **coffee** maker going and offer some additives on the side - Kahlua, RumChata nd the basic Bailey's Irish Cream are gluten-free.

TURKEY DINNER

- Select an **unstuffed turkey**. You <u>cannot</u> choose a stuffed regular turkey and then think you can serve your guest just the meat, not the stuffing. Due to the stuffing containing gluten, this turkey is not safe for a gluten-intolerant person even if they only eat the meat.

- For **potatoes**, we're going for the traditional mashed potatoes. I would suggest Yukon Gold for the best results, but any potato you have available is great. Please see my recipe for mashed potatoes in the Side Dish chapter (page 111) and adjust for the number of people.

- For the first side dish, I'm suggesting **peas,** the frozen kind. They are economical to buy any time of the year and are easy to prepare and delicious. Simply open a package of frozen peas and add to a medium clean pot with water. Boil for about 3 minutes, drain and serve. You can also just place it in the microwave with added water for 3-4 minutes. I find it easiest to let your guests decide how to season them to their taste.

- For the second side dish, I'm suggesting **green beans**. Mix about a pound (450g) of fresh, trimmed green beans in a bowl with 1 tbsp (15 ml) sesame oil, 1 tbsp (15 ml) brown sugar, 1 tsp minced garlic, and 1 tsp garlic chili sauce (if you have some). Toss well and then dump onto a large piece of heavy foil or doubled-up pieces of a thinner foil. Bring the short ends of the foil together and fold to seal, then fold the sides up and seal tightly to make a packet. Cook in the oven with the turkey for 15-20 minutes based on a 325°F (165°C) oven. If your oven is at a higher or lower temperature you may need to adjust the time. You can carefully unwrap the foil packet to check for tenderness. If they require more time, fold them back up and cook for another 5 minutes. Place them into a bowl and sprinkle sesame seeds if desired.

- I would not suggest making **gluten-free buns/rolls** for reasons pointed out in the Roast Beef Dinner section on page 158. If desired, you can ask your gluten-free guest to bring their own as they would know which ones they like best.

- For an additional special side dish, I'm suggesting a gluten-free **Stuffing/Dressing**. There are many different types of dressings so I can't simply say to take your favorite recipe and substitute it with a gluten-free loaf of bread, BUT if you have been following my suggestions on how to keep your kitchen safe and feel comfortable checking ingredients, I would say you can likely just use my tips and how to read a label safely and just alter your favorite recipe. For my dressing recipe, please see the Side Dish chapter (page 121).

- **Gravy** - Since this is a turkey meal with potatoes, you'll want lots of gravy.   You'll likely need to eyeball the amount. It's better to have too much than too little. I would estimate you'll need 1/3-1/2 cup per person. Please see my recipe for gravy in the Side Dish chapter (page 108).

- As for the best part of the meal, you can look at my dessert chapter, but for a turkey meal, I would suggest the **Strawberry Mousse Recipe** (page 143). It is light and easy to make and can be made a day in advance and kept in the fridge until ready.

- Drinks will need to be served before the meal, during the meal, and after. A good option is a **punch** of some kind allowing guests to serve themselves before the meal. Please see my Mocktail Punch recipe (page 153). During the meal itself, a bottle of good **wine** is perfect. I'm certainly not a Sommelier, but based on my internet search, either a full-bodied white wine or a medium-bodied red pairs nicely with turkey. Specifically, a Chardonnay seems to fit the bill. Afterward, get the **coffee** maker going and offer some additives on the side - Kahlua, RumChata and the basic Bailey's Irish Cream flavor are all gluten-free.

- Let's consider the time of year - for Thanksgiving or Christmas an excellent choice is Eggnog - with or without alcohol. For Easter, maybe a colorful Raspberry Sangria. Most are gluten-free, but as always don't assume, please check ingredients.

HOLIDAY TIPS

Here are some extra tips for hosting a complete
dinner no matter if you are 100% gluten-free or
include some gluten dishes.

**Please also refer back to the entire chapter
on TIPS! (page 37)**

- If you have gluten and gluten-free items, please have a **separate, contained area** for whichever dishes are most abundant., i.e. If only a few dishes are gluten-free then the separate area is for the gluten-free dishes. If most of your meal is gluten-free, then the separate area is for gluten dishes. This way your gluten-free guests can prepare their dishes separately and safely from gluten. It is too easy to accidentally put a gluteny spoon in a gluten-free dish. All your hard work to avoid gluten can be ruined by another guest/layperson that doesn't understand the harm of mixing stuff up or cross-contact. They will just go 'oooppss', take the spoon out and put in the right item. They don't realize that they just contaminated an entire gluten-free dish.

  I suggest a separate table (even a little fold-up or kids' table is good) or the far end of your countertop. Please move the gluten dishes far enough away from the gluten-free dishes ensuring that someone won't reach over the gluten-free food with gluten crumbs or exchange serving spoons.

- It's easy to wrap dressing/stuffing in a foil packet to bake in the oven. Whether it's regular or gluten-free, this keeps it contained from anything else. If you are ok with a less formal serving dish you can serve directly in foil too. Otherwise, just dump the foil pack into a serving dish.

- It's easy to cook vegetables in a foil packet in the oven as well. Foil can be used in place of a risky pot or to keep it contained from anything else and again, can be eaten directly out of the foil packet if you're ok with a less formal serving dish. Otherwise, just dump the foil pack into a serving dish.

- Many prepackaged, frozen vegetables in sauces have gluten. Please carefully look at the ingredients or even better, choose to cook plain vegetables. Most frozen vegetables are gluten-free. Please read the packaging.

- Although a pre-packaged salad is convenient, be aware that many contain gluten whether it is the salad ingredients themselves or the dressings. Ones that include croutons, tortillas, or wonton strips are obviously dangerous. Many gluten avoiders will read the package ingredients carefully and can determine the only gluten are croutons and they are in separate packaging, then these can be left out to make a salad gluten-free.   However, sometimes the obvious isn't the only concern.   For example, a Caesar salad has croutons that have gluten, but leaving them off the salad only makes it safe if there are no other gluten ingredients and some Caesar dressings have gluten. Therefore since you are likely less comfortable knowing these things, I suggest you avoid any premade salads unless there are NO gluten ingredients or may contain statements.

- Please be careful with any jarred or bottled pre-made salad dressings. Many have thickening agents and malt vinegar making them unsafe. Reading the ingredients label is key.   You can also make your own dressings assuming you still watch for gluten ingredients in each item.

- Understanding that you may not be cooking gluten-free a lot, it's unrealistic to ask you to buy a new roasting pan. Therefore, think about what you can use to lessen the chance of cross-contact. If you have a stainless steel, coated ceramic, or aluminum pan these work beautifully for roasting and can usually be cleaned easily with soap and water. Stoneware or cast iron are a NO unless they have a nonstick coating, like enamel. If all you have is a porous roasting pan, please carefully use foil to completely wrap around the bottom and up the sides. Any openings or folds in the foil can allow the gluten to sneak in as the juices and fat from the meat roast creep up.   I would bring all ends of the foil up to and over the top of the roasting pan.

- If you're planning to make gluten-free gravy from pan drippings and your roasting pan is safe and was cleaned well, you can make gravy in the pan itself. Otherwise, if you used foil with high sides and no openings you can pour the drippings from the foil-lined roasting pan into a small pot and make gravy in this smooth-sided pot. It is vital that everything remains in the foil though as it is very difficult to pour only the content of foil into another pot without anything underneath the foil also sneaking through. I would suggest you try scooping the contained drippings up with a measuring cup or mug rather than pouring to drippings.

- Please have a new margarine or butter dish and clearly mark it as gluten-free. I would even suggest you don't keep it near anyone that may inadvertently use a knife that may have regular bun crumbs on it.   This can also be your safe source of butter for mashed potatoes or vegetables. Have this butter dish in the gluten-free area and have a separate one in the gluten area.

- Although many Hard (alcoholic) Ciders are safe, you may want to avoid flavored hard ciders, wine coolers or hard lemonade containing malt.

- Although distilled alcohols like vodka, tequila, whiskey, etc. are gluten-free, please consider flavors added after distillation may include gluten ingredients. Alcohol producers are not subject to the same labelling laws, so many companies don't disclose all the ingredients. Sometimes you can find information on the internet, but if you don't know, avoid it.

- Trust me when I state that gluten-free people would rather bring their entire meal than risk getting glutened. Be open if this is their choice. You can provide the details on what steps you have taken or suggest they contribute a dish that might be more difficult for you to provide. i.e. like bring your own buns or make a side dish or a dessert.

- Don't ever assume something will not have gluten. I have seen many turkeys that are injected with seasonings that may or do contain gluten.

Always check ingredients! Always check ingredients!

<u>APPENDIX</u>

<u>What to tell your GF guest(s)?</u>

<u>Please remember</u> -

As mentioned quite a few times in this book, don't be frustrated if a gluten-free guest does not trust your meal, no matter how many extra steps you take to make it safe for them. You have no idea how they react or what kind of problems they have had in the past. In addition, you can't control other guest's actions during your meal. It is always best to check with your gluten-free guest. You can even tell them you followed advice from this book and even show them the book.

For those that dine with you!

I would suggest you tell them that although the meal was made in a non-gluten-free house, special care and attention was given to avoiding gluten. All ingredients were doubled checked for gluten ingredients and allergen warnings. All surfaces, utensils, and pots/pans were washed with a clean cloth and dish soap before use and parchment paper or foil was used for extra protection in pans. You can add that you took extra care to ensure that the gluten-free food is separated from gluten dishes to ensure they stay safe from cross-contact.

What to attach to your dish when you're not around to answer questions!

(You have my permission to plagiarize the following statement:)

Although these treats were made in a non-gluten-free house, special care and attention was given to avoiding gluten. All ingredients and allergen statements were doubled checked for gluten. All surfaces, utensils, and pots/pans were washed with a clean cloth and dish soap before use and parchment paper was used for extra protection. They have been stored in an airtight container since. Enjoy!

Parchment Paper Tips

Parchment paper, also called baking paper, is extremely handy in protecting food from potential gluten sources. It can be used on baking sheets, inside cake pans, and on other baking containers to act as a barrier between the dish and the food being baked or cooked. It also keeps food from sticking and makes food much easier to remove once they've been cooked. Don't mix up the parchment paper with wax paper though. Wax paper should NOT go in the oven, whereas parchment paper can go in the oven up to **425 °F (220 °C).**

Although you don't need to worry too much, there is a correct side to use. Did you know the shinier side should always be facing up when baking because it creates a better seal?

No matter which method you choose for lining your pan, a little tip to keep the parchment paper itself from slipping, is to spray just a little bit of cooking spray in the pan before adding the parchment or just add a little butter or grease to the corners.

Square or Rectangle Dish Method 1 - preferred

Put your pan on a piece of parchment that is 2-3" (4-8 cm) larger than each side of the pan. Then cut a diagonal slit in each corner of the paper towards the corners of the pan. (**Images A ,B and C**) This creates two flaps at each corner, which are important to making the paper fit. Once you place the paper in the pan, when you press it into the corners the paper should fold nicely in place. (**Images D and E**)

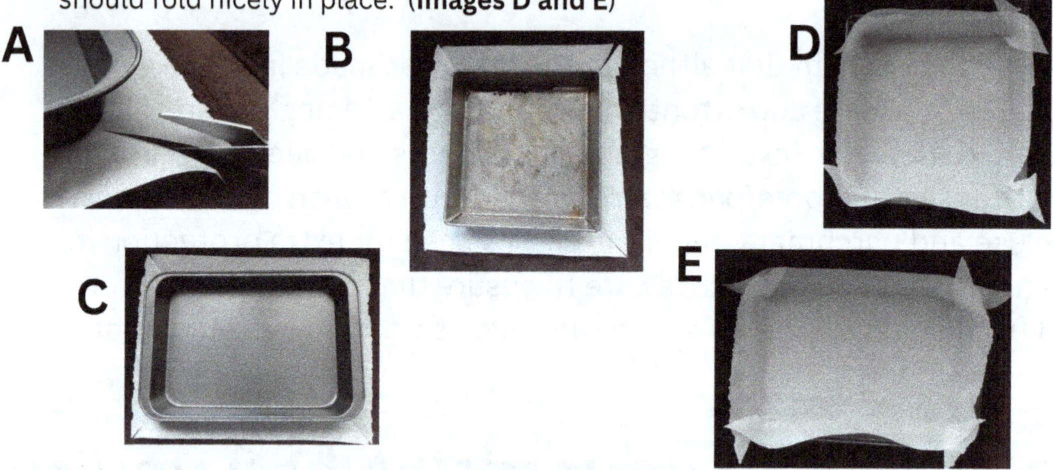

Square or Rectangle Dish Method 2

NOTE - I only recommend this method if your pan is clean and free from potential gluten. This method uses separate pieces of parchment and therefore does **NOT** complete a seal from potential gluten in the corners. If you think your pan is too dirty to be safe, please follow method 1 above. Cut a piece of parchment paper that is long enough for the edges of the paper to extend out the edge of tray 2 - 3" (4-8.cm), but is only as wide as the pan the other way. (**Image F**) Then cut a second piece of parchment paper to go in the opposite direction across the tray ensuring that all the edges are covered (**Images G**). You may need 2 pieces going in the same direction for rectangular pans (**Image H**)

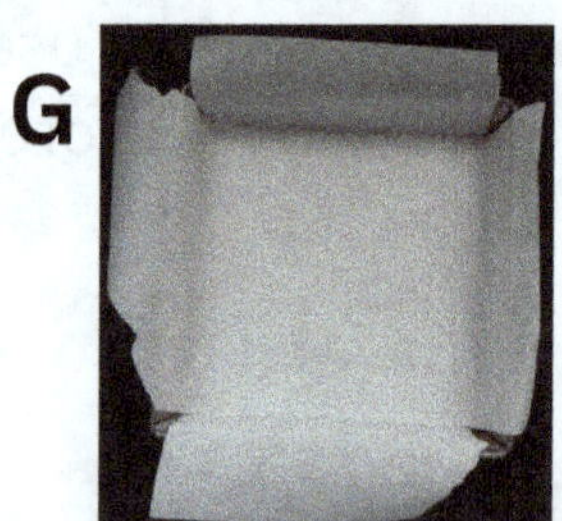

Circular dish/pan

For a round or circular pan, cut a piece of parchment paper the size of the bottom of the pan. (**Image I**). I like to place the pan on the paper and just draw around the pan. Then cut paper with scissors. Just mark the side that faces down so it doesn't contact the food.

Then take a strip of paper that is slightly higher than the sides of the pan and as long as necessary to go all the way around the dish. You'll likely need to use a spray to hold the paper in this method. (**Image J**)

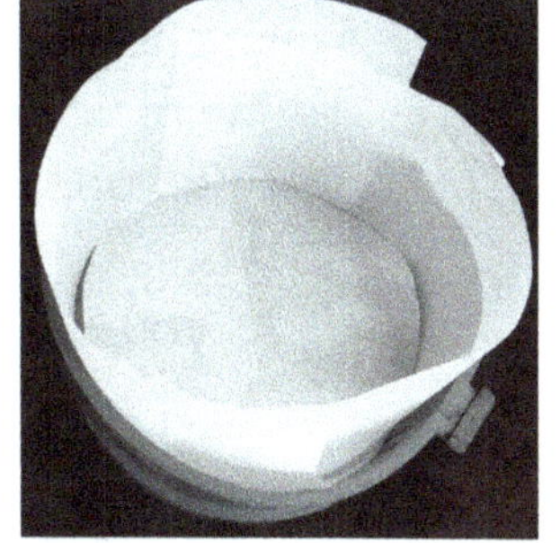

Please note however, as the parchment paper will be in 2 pieces it will **not** be a complete barrier to gluten. If you think your pan is too dirty to be safe, just follow the steps below for a roasting pan. The finished edges of what you bake will not be as smooth, but it will be safer from gluten.

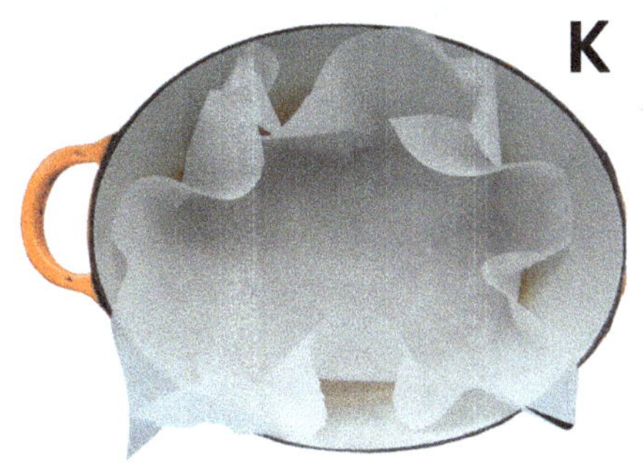

Roasting pan

Since anything cooked in a roasting pan is less likely to need a smooth, attractive edge, you can simply take a large piece of paper that covers the bottom, but goes up the sides of pan and push it into pan.   (**Image K**) There is no need to worry about the sides crinkling up.   Your meat will hold it in place.

Muffin Pans (If you don't have paper cup liners/cases)

Cut twelve - 5" (13 cm) squares of parchment square for each tin. (**Image L**) Place one square into each hole, and then press them down with your hands or a thin glass, so that the bottom creases around the edges of the tin. (**Image M**) Your paper liner is now ready for batter (**Image N**)

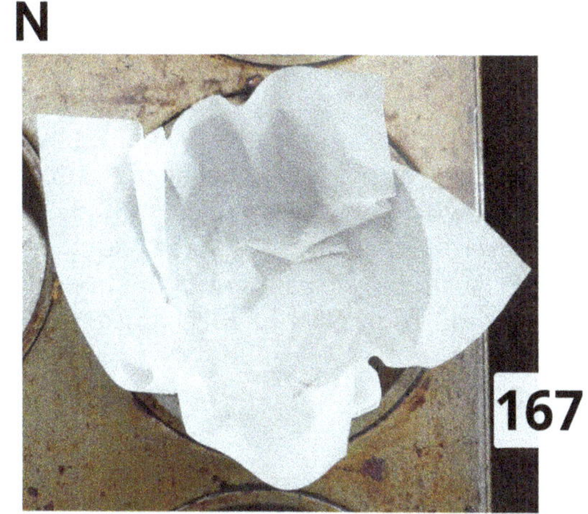

ACKNOWLEDGEMENTS

Creating a cookbook is a multi-faceted process that requires a combination of culinary skills, photography skills, writing and design skills, and the ability to research, test, and refine recipes. This can be a challenging task. Although my concept for this book was decided upon early, the research and selection of recipes that aligned with my theme wasn't easy.

As you can imagine this is difficult for one person to do therefore, I would like to acknowledge the following:

- I'd like to first thank my family for their support and understanding while I created this book. I made them try a lot of recipes to decide what works best.   Although the ones I included in this book were well received, others were not as delicious. There were many times they had to wait to eat while I set up the camera and equipment to get the perfect shot.

- I'd like to thank my youngest daughter Kendal, for her assistance with the photography. She took pictures, held my equipment, provided suggestions for staging, let me know what she liked and didn't like. It wasn't the most fun a child can have and I appreciated the help. Kendal was also a model in some of my pictures.

- I'd like to thank my oldest daughter, Sophie, for eating many dishes when she is not a lover of casseroles or cheesy toppings. She also worked as a model in some of the photos. She followed my instructions well and even listened to me for a change.

- Although I have been making most of these recipes for a while, they were all once original recipes created by someone else. If I knew where I first got the recipe from I would certainly state it, but I would like to thank all the many recipe creators out there that continue to make recipes available that are gluten-free and delicious.

- Most of the photographs used throughout the book are my personal photos. However, a few photos and the graphics are taken from or designed in canva.com and I have made attribution where appropriate.

- A huge thank you to all the people that provided genuine feedback and reviews on this book before publishing. I appreciated the time each person took to read and respond.

- Thank you to my editors - A. J. Seymour and Richard Vanden Berg for your knowledge and hard work in finding my mistakes.

- The information found in the beginning part of this book and what was researched on regulations in foreign countries was attained from many sources but mainly:
  - USA - https://nationalceliac.org/celiac-disease-resources/confusing-gluten-free-diet-ingredients/
  - USA Food Labeling Modernization Act of 2021 (FLMA) - https://www.congress.gov/bill/117th-congress/house-bill/4917
  - Canada - https://www.canada.ca/en/health-canada/services/food-allergies-intolerances/avoiding-allergens-food/allergen-labelling.html
  - U.K. - https://www.coeliac.org.uk/food-businesses/brands-and-manufacturers/gluten-free-and-the-law/#:~:text=Communicating%20gluten%20free-,To%20label%20gluten%20free%20on%20your%20products%20you%20need%20to,a%20separate%20piece%20of%20legislation.
  - Australia - https://www.foodstandards.gov.au/consumer/labelling/Pages/allergen-labelling.aspx and https://www.coeliac.org.au/s/the-gluten-free-diet

169